Jesus Loves You and Evolution Is True

Jesus Loves You and Evolution Is True

Why Youth Ministry Needs Science

Sara Sybesma Tolsma and Jason Lief

FORTRESS PRESS
MINNEAPOLIS

JESUS LOVES YOU AND EVOLUTION IS TRUE

Why Youth Ministry Needs Science

Copyright © 2019 Fortress Press, an imprint of 1517 Media. All rights reserved. Except for brief quotations in critical articles or reviews, no part of this book may be reproduced in any manner without prior written permission from the publisher. Email copyright@1517.media or write to Permissions, Fortress Press, PO Box 1209, Minneapolis, MN 55440-1209.

Cover design: Lauren Williamson

Print ISBN: 978-1-5064-3973-0

eBook ISBN: 978-1-5064-4012-5

The paper used in this publication meets the minimum requirements of American National Standard for Information Sciences — Permanence of Paper for Printed Library Materials, ANSI Z329.48-1984.

Manufactured in the U.S.A.

From Jason:
This book is dedicated to my children:
Naomi, Christian, and Savannah.
Always remember that true Christian faith
is never afraid of asking hard questions.

From Sara:
For Jeff, Ellen, Joseph, and Daniel
for their unwavering love, support,
and encouragement.

Contents

	Introduction: Asking Good Questions Jason Lief	1
1.	Making Connections: Science *and* Faith Sara Sybesma Tolsma	5
2.	Baseball and Barth: Why Youth Ministry Needs Evolution Jason Lief	31
3.	Adam and Lucy: What Evolution Says about Being Human Sara Sybesma Tolsma	57
4.	The Cross and Creation: Saint Francis, Evolution, and the Love of God Jason Lief	81
5.	Tending the Garden: What Evolution Says about Our Future Sara Sybesma Tolsma	105
6.	Jesus Can Hit a Curve Ball: What It Means to Be Made in the Image of God Jason Lief	139
7.	When Darwin Wept: Redeeming Suffering and Death Sara Sybesma Tolsma	167

8. Embracing Our Animal: Youth Ministry in a Secular₃ World   193
   Jason Lief

Epilogue   217
Jason Lief

Introduction: Asking Good Questions
Jason Lief

Recently, some youth-ministry college students spent time talking with high schoolers about their views on science and faith. The purpose was to get a snapshot of what young people believe, so we asked about their views of the Bible, their interpretation of the Genesis creation accounts, what they thought of evolution, and even whether they would ever get a tattoo. Most of the time, they gave us what they thought we wanted—evolution is bad, and the Bible is completely true in everything it says. At one church, I asked if anyone wondered if evolution might be true. Silence. Out of the corner of my eye I noticed an adult sponsor elbowing a young person. Finally, the young woman raised her hand and said, "Fine, I believe evolution is true." "Thank you!" I replied, and then I asked her to elaborate. She started talking about her science class, the evidence she finds convincing, and how taking science seriously has led to important breakthroughs in medicine and technology. I asked if this made her question her faith, and she hesitated. "Sometimes," she said. "I hear about how we're not supposed to believe in evolution, or evolution is bad, and it makes me wonder—maybe the Bible isn't true."

Through our visits we heard many different stories and listened to many different perspectives. Some students say they don't struggle with science and faith, either because they don't really care about science or they just accept what their church or family teaches them about the

Bible. Others, however, exhibited more tension. The most important comment we heard is that young people want the church to talk about science and faith more. As various studies have shown, this topic is crucial for those worried about young people leaving the church.

Most discussions about evolution and faith focus on the creation accounts in Genesis. We've decided to take a different approach, focusing instead on the incarnation. Christians believe that in Jesus Christ, God became a human being. What does this say about the relationship between faith and science? What does this say about the relationship between God and creation? The incarnation forces the church to take the created, material world seriously, which has a direct effect on youth ministry. Increasingly, young people live in a world of abstraction. Everything from social media to virtual reality, to grades, to Spotify pushes young people away from their embodied reality into a hyperspiritualized way of life. The church doesn't help, at times overemphasizing doctrine, morality, and new forms of spirituality that tend to leave our bodies behind. Not only does the faith-and-science discussion have important consequences for the faith of young people, it also has important consequences on how they understand what it means to be human living in this world.

This book is a conversation on the importance of evolution for the church and for youth ministry. It is a dialogue that recognizes theology and biology are two different ways of making sense of the world, but there are important places of intersection, or transversal spaces, that allow us to talk with each other. Sara writes as a biologist who is also a Christian, taking seriously what we can know about the world by looking closely at the various forms of biological life. I write as a practical theologian, engaging theological views of the incarnation, salvation, and creation by looking at Scripture and theology. We both believe there are important connections between biology and theology when it comes to the faith life of the Christian community, and the faith life of young people in particular. Our hope is to point out the transversal spaces that exist between theology and biology so the Christian community might see how the science-and-faith issue is not an either/or choice. The incarnation necessarily means it is a both/and endeavor, and our task as the Christian community is to help young people live into the beautiful mystery of incarnation that is at the center of Christian faith. For dialogue to happen, biology and theology need to pose questions to each other. This cannot just be theology asking questions of science or trying to fit science into the worldview of the Bible; it must be a true dialogue whereby theology and biology challenge and inform each other.

In the first chapter, Sara will provide evidence for evolution, focusing on how the creation is open to the future. Jason will then explore what it means to see the incarnation as the culmination of creation and how this changes the way we think about our embodied humanity. This will be followed up with a chapter in which Sara will examine the evidence for human evolution, specifically focusing on what evolution says about what it means to be human. In the fourth chapter, Jason will explore what it means to see the act of creation and incarnation together as an expression of God's love. In chapter 5, Sara will argue that evolution provides a way for thinking about the relational connections of our humanity with the created world—that what it means to be human is to be deeply connected to creation. Jason will follow up with a chapter that presents a theological anthropology—a biblical and theological understanding of what it means to be human in the light of the incarnation and the findings of science. In chapter 7, Sara will focus on what it all means—how evolution describes a creation that moves from death to new life. To conclude, Jason will focus on what this conversation means for youth ministry—how a conversation between evolution and theology can help young people live into their identity as the new humanity of Jesus Christ.

Our hope is that this book will contribute to the important conversation on the relationship between science and faith, and that it will encourage others to approach these issues with humility and generosity. The Christian community needs to have healthy conversations about evolution and faith so young people know they don't have to make a choice between the two.

1.

Making Connections: Science *and* Faith

Sara Sybesma Tolsma

> One of the basic rules of the universe is that nothing is perfect. Perfection simply doesn't exist. . . . Without imperfection, neither you nor I would exist.[1]
>
> —Stephen Hawking

Peter's Quest

Peter recounted his personal journey with faith and science at a recent conference I attended. He was raised in a church that condemned evolutionary theory as something only atheists believe. His church taught that to be a faithful follower of God, he needed to choose between faith and science. His pastor taught that either God created the world in six twenty-four-hour days or the Bible was wrong, and therefore untrustworthy. His youth-group leader agreed—everyone had to choose. Faith *or* science.

Peter was a curious student who loved science, so the message from his church caused him anxiety. In high-school biology class, he was confronted with the evidence for evolution. He saw the data supporting a 4.5-billion-

---

1. Maria Vultaggio, "16 Inspirational Stephen Hawking Quotes about Life, the Universe and More," *Newsweek*, March 14, 2018, https://tinyurl.com/yaf-flko2.

year-old Earth. He encountered the evidence showing how species changed over time. It left Peter feeling confused. The evidence made sense, so he wanted to know more. He began reading books on the origins of biological life and, against the advice of his family and his church, studied biology at the university near his home. He joined a research group that explored the genetic changes that take place when cells become cancerous. The work was exciting and rewarding, and he was good at it. His research on cancer cells gave him a window into the conserved processes in cells from widely divergent organisms—something best explained by evolutionary theory. He presented his research at a national meeting and published his work in a peer-reviewed journal. He was thrilled when he won a prestigious award for excellence in undergraduate research. During his senior year, Peter was accepted to a PhD program in genetics at a prominent graduate school where he studied gene regulation in yeast.

Through the years, Peter did not forget what his pastor taught: that he had to choose between science and faith. As he learned more about biology, he became convinced of the overwhelming scientific evidence for evolutionary theory. If he had to make a choice, like so many others, Peter chose science over his Christian faith.

At this conference, Peter expressed his gratitude that we serve a relentlessly persistent God. After years spent rejecting his faith, Peter began to search for something to fill the deep emptiness he could not shake. A friend suggested that maybe his church was wrong and that having to choose between science and faith was a false choice. Intrigued, he began reading again. This time, he looked for books by Christians who were open to connections between faith and science. He attended a church that made space for doubt and questions. Through the patient grace of a God who pursued him through his doubts, a community of faithful Christians, and the hard work of reading, learning, and listening, Peter found his way back to faith. In doing so, he discovered a deep connection that allowed him to hold on to both Christianity and science.

This story plays out repeatedly in the lives of young people raised in churches that give young people the false choice between faith *or* science; unfortunately, not all of them find their way back like Peter. Thankfully, the story does not have to unfold this way. Helping Christian young people see the connections between faith and science can go a long way in changing the narrative. That's exactly what this book is about—exploring the meaningful connections between Christian faith and evolution. One of those connections is the intersection of evolution and incarnation. We hope this book can launch meaningful dialogue between science and faith that leads Christian young people to view faith and science as harmonious. When young people understand science and faith in harmony, we believe that we can change the way the story goes.

What Is Evolutionary Theory?

Charles Darwin formally proposed the theory of evolution in his 1859 book, *The Origin of Species*.[2] It is a misconception, however, to assume that evolutionary theory originated with Darwin's book. For decades, geologists and paleontologists were uncovering convincing evidence that the earth was old, that life was also old, and that life had changed over time. Fossil evidence revealed species that

---

2. Charles Darwin, *On the Origin of Species by Means of Natural Selection, or the Preservation of Favoured Races in the Struggle for Life* (London: John Murray, 1859).

used to exist but were now extinct. Embryologists and anatomists were discovering common pathways of development and the structural consistencies that underlie evolutionary theory. Darwin's book made such an impact because it gathered all the evidence of the time into one volume to support the claim that species evolved from a common ancestor. The change he described is often called *descent with modification*.[3] Darwin's book was also important because he proposed a plausible mechanism by which life could evolve: natural selection. Natural selection is the "preservation of favourable individual differences and variations, and the destruction of those which are injurious."[4] This means that certain changes will help a species survive and reproduce in an environment, while other changes mean they will be at greater risk of dying.

Evolution, in its most basic sense, is simply *change over time*: changes in the average characteristics or traits of a population of interbreeding individuals.[5] Within a population, individuals differ in traits due to genetic differences. Genetic differences arise because the enzyme that copies DNA makes mistakes, and these mistakes lead to changes. These changes are called *mutations*. Mutations create variants, or alleles—genes that differ slightly in their sequence. Over time, variants accumulate in individuals and their descendants, which leads to a genetically diverse popu-

---

3. Darwin, *Origin of Species*, 480.
4. Darwin, *Origin of Species*, 481; see also Charles Darwin and Alfred Wallace, "On the Tendency of Species to Form Varieties; and on the Perpetuation of Varieties and Species by Natural Means of Selection.," *Journal of the Proceedings of the Linnean Society of London. Zoology* 3, no. 9 (August 1, 1858): 45–62, https://doi.org/10.1111/j.1096-3642.1858.tb02500.x.
5. Paul Copan, Tremper Longman III, Christopher L. Reese, and Michael G. Strauss, eds., *Dictionary of Christianity and Science: The Definitive Reference for the Intersection of Christian Faith and Contemporary Science* (Grand Rapids: Zondervan, 2017), 226.

lation. If the population reproduces sexually, the mixing of maternal and paternal DNA during fertilization results in new combinations of alleles, which adds to the genetic diversity of the population even more.

Evolutionary theory or Darwinian evolution is a *scientific* explanation or theory for the emergence of the diversity of life from a common ancestor through variation and natural selection over approximately four billion years. The theory is well tested and has broad explanatory power. As a scientific theory, it does not and cannot speak to purpose, and this is often a source of misunderstanding. The terms *Darwinism* and *evolutionism* have come to mean *philosophical naturalism*—a belief that includes purposelessness. Philosophical naturalism is not a scientific theory testable using the scientific method and should not be conflated with evolutionary theory. Most scientists who are Christians would agree that evolutionary theory or Darwinian evolution is consistent with orthodox Christianity, but Darwinism, evolutionism, and philosophical naturalism are not.

Scientific Theories

One of the common concerns expressed by those who doubt evolutionary theory is the use of the word *theory*. "It's only a theory" is a complaint that opponents often raise. This concern reveals a misunderstanding of the scientific use of the term *theory*, as well as a misunderstanding of the scientific method. In everyday speech, the word *theory* is used differently than in a scientific context. In informal speaking, a person might say, "I have a theory as to why Joan went to the café yesterday afternoon. She was hoping to run into Bruce." This use of the word *theory* demands very little evidence. In fact, you might substitute the word *hunch* for *theory*. In a scientific context, the word *theory* cannot be replaced by the word *hunch*. The word *theory*, in a scientific context, is a weighty word. It only applies to ideas that have been tested and supported over and over through experiments and observation. Theories are supported by evidence accumulated through the scientific method. Theories have broad explanatory power; they must explain how a part of the natural world works.

The scientific method is a process by which an idea can become a theory. In the scientific method, scientists make an observation, and based on that observation they propose a statement, called a *hypothesis*, that explains what has been observed. Predictions emerge from the hypothesis as a way for a scientist to anticipate how a system will behave, assuming the evidence supports the hypothesis. The scientist then designs experiments to test the hypothesis using those predictions, performs the experiments, and analyzes the results. If the experimental results are consistent with the predictions, the hypothesis is supported. Notice that I did not use the word *prove*. Hypotheses are not proven, they are only supported. This might seem indecisive, but, in reality, it keeps scientists open to the possibility that their hypothesis might not be completely accurate. It maintains a level of intellectual humility necessary for the scientific method to work. Every experiment has the potential to alter a hypothesis, and good scientists know they must always be open to the possibility that their understanding of how the natural world works might be incomplete. After scientists test a hypothesis many times, they publish the results so other scientists can see their data, read their interpretations, and assess for themselves whether their claims are justified. Scientists in similar fields will use these results to inform their own experiments, so, after publication, a hypothesis is retested by other scientists in other laboratories. Many times, these scientists are in direct competition with the scientist who published the original results, which means they are highly motivated to find flaws in the interpretation or experimental design. This rigorous analysis of data is why the scientific method is so successful at discovering truth. Any individual report or set of reports may not produce a hypothesis that is completely accurate. However, over time, when many scientists in many laboratories work through this process, a hypothesis becomes closer to the truth, while always remaining open to the possibility of revision. When a hypothesis has been tested many times, using many methods, by many different scientists, and it has widespread implications with great explanatory power, then a hypothesis graduates to the level of a theory. In a scientific context, theories are a big deal!

The cell theory is a good example. It states that:

- Cells are the basic structural and functional unit of life.
- All living organisms are comprised of one or more cells.
- All cells come from preexisting cells.

Does anyone today dispute the cell theory? Yet, it is *just* a theory.

This weighty use of the word theory applies to evolutionary theory. Evolutionary theory is a hypothesis that has broad explanatory power and for which scientists have accumulated so much supporting evidence that it has graduated to the rank of theory. You may feel like you have seen something like this before if you are a fan of legal dramas on television. The accumulation of evidence for a hypothesis and eventually a theory looks a bit like a jury trial.

When a trial is over and a jury hands down a verdict, you rarely, if ever, prove that a defendant was guilty or innocent. Rather, the jury weighs the evidence and the evidence points the jury in the direction of guilty or not guilty. More evidence makes a jury more confident in their decision.

The story of peppered moths offers a good example of how the scientific method works to build and revise theories. The *typica* form of peppered moths have white wings with specks of black. This coloring is ideal for camouflaging from predators on lichen-covered tree trunks. Peppered moths can experience a random mutation that leads to melanization. Melanized moths, the *carbonaria* form, have wings that are mostly black. Black moths are highly visible on white, lichen-covered tree trunks. Birds looking for a tasty snack quickly eat these easy targets, so random, dark-colored variants have little time to survive or reproduce, rarely passing their new allele on to succeeding generations. During the Industrial Revolution, however, peppered moths changed dramatically. The population started as almost entirely *typica* but, in a few decades, shifted to mostly *carbonaria*. Scientists hypothesized that this change was due to natural selection. During the Industrial Revolution, the environment changed. Lichen on tree bark absorbed pollutants pumped into the air from factories, turning the lichen from mostly white to mostly black. In this new environment, random melanized variant peppered moths were camouflaged and the *typica* white moths stood out to predatory birds like a neon sign. The advantage was reversed in this changed environment. A trait that was an imperfection under previous conditions was an opportunity during the Industrial Revolution. In the new environment, melanized moths survived and reproduced while hungry birds quickly ate the white *typica* moths.[6]

---

6. C. A. Clarke, G. S. Mani, and G. Wynne, "Evolution in Reverse: Clean Air

In the early twenty-first century, scientists began questioning the established explanation for the shift in the peppered moth population from mostly *typica* to mostly *carbonaria*. For almost a decade, scientists scrutinized the original work. They performed new experiments, using new techniques that could either support or refute the established explanation. As a result of a six-year study of bird predation using almost five thousand moths, a group of scientists confirmed the original conclusion that differential camouflage and bird predation were the most important factors in the decline of the *typica* form and subsequent rise of the *carbonaria* form during industrialization.[7] The study also documented a reversal (back to more *typica* and fewer *carbonaria* forms) after environmental regulations reduced the level of pollutants in the air, further supporting the original explanation. Another group of scientists discovered the gene variant that caused melanization.[8] They used molecular genetics to confirm that the *typica* variant was an old one and that the *carbonaria* variant arose recently and rapidly spread because of strong natural selection. After careful reexamination using new and old techniques, the additional data added support to the original hypothesis.[9]

    and the Peppered Moth," *Biological Journal of the Linnean Society* 26, no. 2 (October 1985): 189–99, https://doi.org/10.1111/j.1095-8312.1985.tb01555.x.

7. L. M. Cook, B. S. Grant, I. J. Saccher, and J. Mallet, "Selective Bird Predation on the Peppered Moth: The Last Experiment of Michael Majerus," *Biology Letters*, February 8, 2012, https://doi.org/10.1098/rsbl.2011.1136.

8. Argen van't Hof, N. Edmonds, M. Dalikova, F. Marec, and I. J. Saccheri, "Industrial Melanism in British Peppered Moths Has a Singular and Recent Mutational Origin," *Science* 332, no. 6032 (2011): 958–60.

9. L. M. Cook and I. J. Saccheri, "The Peppered Moth and Industrial Melanism: Evolution of a Natural Selection Case Study," *Heredity* 110, no. 3 (March

Did these experiments prove the hypothesis? No. In biology, hypotheses are only strengthened. Enough experimental evidence for a hypothesis that has broad explanatory power moves a hypothesis to the status of theory. While the experimental evidence for the peppered moth hypothesis might be adequate for the status of theory, the hypothesis does not have explanatory power that is broad enough to achieve the state of theory. Rather, the peppered-moth hypothesis supports evolutionary theory. Changes in pigmentation, like scientists observed in the peppered moths, are minor changes that occurred over a relatively short time. The two forms of moth, *carbonaria* and *typica*, are variants of the same species. However, if a population experiences habitat fragmentation or becomes separated by a geological barrier, minor changes can accumulate over a long time, leading to such genetic divergence in the two populations that they form two distinct species with a common ancestry.

Evidence for Evolution

Evolution is an extremely well-supported scientific theory and, like a verdict handed down with confidence, includes many lines of evidence, a variety of experimental approaches, and an assessment of the problem from different angles, all of which point to a similar conclusion. Supporting evidence for evolutionary theory comes from astronomy, geology, anatomy, biogeography, archeology, developmental biology, and genetics.

When comparative anatomists examine the structures of various animals, they see remarkable similarities. Frogs,

2013): 207–12, https://doi.org/10.1038/hdy.2012.92; van't Hof et al., "Industrial Melanism," 958–60.

cats, lizards, and bats have forelimbs used for very different functions—jumping, running, crawling, and flying. The outward appearance of the forelimbs of these diverse animals is also quite different, yet the bone structure for all four are very similar. All four have a relatively thick upper bone called the humerus and two lighter forearm bones called the radius and ulna. Fossils, including transitional fossils, have the same skeletal structure as these animals. Organisms that seem quite divergent not only have common arm bones, but they also share carpals (wrist bones), metacarpals (hand bones), and phalanges (finger bones) (Figure 1.1). These kinds of anatomical similarities are not limited to limbs but can be seen throughout animal anatomy.

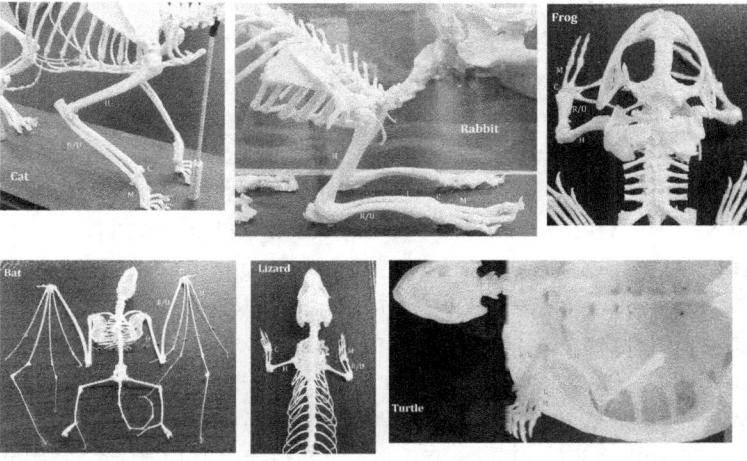

Figure 1.1. The upper limb bones from six different vertebrates: cat, rabbit, frog, bat, lizard, and turtle. The animals in this figure use their upper limbs differently—to walk, crawl, hop, swim, fly—yet the basic bone structures are analogous. Labels: humerus (H), radius and ulna (R/U), carpals (C), and metacarpals and phalanges (M).

If you have been to a natural history museum, you know that scientists use fossil evidence to support evolutionary theory. The fossil record, locations of fossils in rock layers, and radiometric dating help scientists look back over time to understand what organisms were present at various times. Evolutionary theory predicts that, in addition to fossils of organisms that have gone extinct and fossils that are similar to modern organisms, scientists should find transitional fossils. Transitional fossils represent life-forms that have traits of both ancestral organisms and the modern organisms descended from them. Cetacea provide examples of transitional fossils. Cetaceans include whales, dolphins, and porpoises, although scientists often use the word *whales* to refer to the whole order. Whales give birth to live, placental young, which they nurse with milk from mammary glands, and they have hair, jaws consisting of a single bone, three middle ear bones, and lungs, all of which places them firmly within the Mammalia family. They are unique mammals in that they are aquatic. From an evolutionary perspective, this means the closest evolutionary relatives of whales are terrestrial. Scientists predicted that if they transitioned from terrestrial animals, then there must be transitional fossils showing characteristics of animals that transformed from land-dwelling organisms to ocean-dwelling Cetaceans. Scientists could test this prediction when they discovered Cetacean fossils thirty years ago.[10] Since then, scientists have uncovered so much fossil evidence for whale evolution that it is now one of the best-known examples of transitional fossil evidence in support of evolutionary theory.[11]

10. S. Bajpai, J. G. M. Thewissen, and A. Sahni, "The Origin and Early Evolution of Whales: Macroevolution Documented on the Indian Subcontinent," *Journal of Biosciences* 34, no. 5 (November 2009): 673–86.
11. Annalisa Berta, James L. Sumich, and Kit M. Kovacs, *Marine Mammals:*

In Darwin's original edition of *The Origin of Species*, he suggested that whales evolved from bears. After people ridiculed this suggestion, Darwin removed it from later editions. While Darwin was incorrect in suggesting that whales evolved from bears, he was correct in that whales did evolve from land animals. We now know that whales evolved from small deer-like mammals that lived in the Himalayas.[12] The fossil record documents transitional animals that exhibit the morphological changes connecting ancient hooved mammals to modern whales. One change that scientists have examined carefully is the anatomical components necessary for hearing. All mammals have middle ear bones in the tympanic portion of the temporal bone of the skull and an opening in their mandible (lower jawbone) called the mandibular foramen through which blood vessels and nerves run. Modern whales have a unique modification of these structures. The foramen is much larger and deeper, housing a fat pad that conducts sound from the jaw to the middle ear. In short, the mandibular foramen in modern whales is a necessary part of their hearing apparatus. Evolutionary theory predicts that transitional fossils would show anatomical changes that transition from a small, shallow mandibular foramen that houses only blood vessels and nerves to the unique structure we see in modern whales. This is precisely what scientists observed when

Evolutionary Biology (London: Academic Press, 2015); Annalisa Berta, *The Rise of Marine Mammals: 50 Million Years of Evolution* (Baltimore: John Hopkins University Press, 2017); J. G. M. Thewissen and Sunil Bajpai, "Whale Origins as a Poster Child for Macroevolution," *Bioscience* 51, no. 12 (December 2001): 1037–49; J. G. M. Thewissen, Lisa Noelle Cooper, Mark T. Clementz, Sunil Bajpai, and B. N. Tiwari, "Whales Originated from Aquatic Artiodactyls in the Eocene Epoch of India," *Nature* 450, no. 7173 (December 20, 2007): 1190–94, https://doi.org/10.1038/nature06343.

12. Bajpai, Thewissen, and Sahni, "Origin and Early Evolution of Whales."

they finally discovered the transitional fossils.[13] These transitional fossils also exhibited the predicted intermediate structures for the positions of eye sockets and nasal openings, the morphology of molars, and the anatomy of limbs and girdles.[14] Scientists uncovered fossils that, when put together in chronological order, told a story that revealed a gradual evolution from a terrestrial hooved mammal to aquatic mammals.

Cetacean physiology tells a similar story. Land mammals require a source of fresh water to rid their bodies of excess salt. Whales, however, are able to survive without fresh water because their physiology uses water sparingly and they produce highly concentrated urine. Evolutionary theory predicts that this transition to freshwater independence evolved gradually, and scientists found evidence to confirm this prediction.

Bones and teeth contain phosphate (PO_4^{-3}), and the oxygen in phosphate is a reflection of the drinking behavior of an animal as it made and remodeled its bones and teeth. Because fresh water and seawater contain different levels of oxygen isotopes and because the animals use these oxygen isotopes to build bones and teeth, scientists can distinguish the type of water an animal drank by measuring the oxygen isotope composition in teeth or bones. As predicted, the oldest fossils in this lineage show isotope levels expected for animals that depended on fresh water along with anatomy that is consistent with a terrestrial or shal-

---

13. J. G. M. Thewissen, E. M. Williams, L. J. Roe, and S. T. Hussain, "Skeletons of Terrestrial Cetaceans and the Relationship of Whales to Artiodactyls," *Nature* 413 (September 20, 2001): 277; Thewissen and Bajpai, "Whale Origins as a Poster Child."

14. Alexandra Houssaye, Paul Tafforeau, Christian de Muizon, and Philip D. Gingerich, "Transition of Eocene Whales from Land to Sea: Evidence from Bone Microstructure," *PLoS ONE* 10, no. 2 (2015): https://doi.org/10.1371/journal.pone.0118409.

low-water habitat. Younger fossils exhibit isotope levels consistent with a life cycle in which at least part of the animal's life was associated with fresh water. These animals may have used fresh water for drinking but lived in the sea or lived in fresh water during the early part of their life, while teeth mineralized, and migrated to the sea as adults. The youngest fossils and modern cetaceans have anatomy and oxygen isotope levels indicative of a completely marine life.[15] The physiological evidence from transitional fossils is consistent with the anatomical evidence for a move from terrestrial to aquatic environments.

Another area in which evolutionary theory makes testable predictions is biogeography. Biogeography is the study of the distribution of species on earth. It is closely connected to plate tectonics, a geological theory that the earth's crust is divided into plates that move slowly over the mantle. Plate tectonics and biogeography are connected because throughout the history of earth, when continents collide, species mix, and when continents separate, they separate species into isolated groups. Biogeographers study the effects of species distribution taking the movement of continents into account. Evolutionary theory predicts that related species should be found on different continents if plate tectonic theory suggests they were once adjacent to one another. Geologists know that Africa, South America, Australia, and New Zealand once formed a supercontinent called Gondwanaland. Plate tectonics theory provides evidence that individual continents separated from Gondwanaland at different times. Africa separated first, then New Zealand, and lastly Australia and South America

---

15. J. G. M. Thewissen, L. J. Roe, J. R. O'Neil, S. T. Hussain, A. Sahni, and S. Bajpai, "Evolution of Cetacean Osmoregulation," *Nature* 381 (May 30, 1996): 379.

separated.[16] If species were present on the supercontinent Gondwanaland, they should exhibit relationships that reflect this geological history. One species that reveals these biogeographical relationships is the Gondwanan midge, small flies. Scientists measured the evolutionary relationships between midges from different parts of the world using morphology and molecular genetics.[17] Midges in South America and Australia are more closely related to one another than they are to midges found in New Zealand. All three of these midges are more closely related to each other than they are to midges found in Africa. The morphological and genetic relationships between midges precisely mirror the order in which the continents separated and confirm what scientists predict based on this geological history.

How developmental patterns evolve provides another important line of evidence for evolutionary theory. Early work in this area, often called EvoDevo to signify the relationship between *evo*lutionary theory and *deve*lopmental biology, relied on structure or morphology to group similar organisms. More recently, EvoDevo intersects with molecular genetics since patterns of gene expression underlie the mechanisms of developmental biology. Early observations of morphological similarities included similarities in body patterning or plans. Some organisms exhibit embryonic

16. Annelise Frazão, Hélio Ricardo da Silva, and Claudia Augusta de Moraes Russo, "The Gondwana Breakup and the History of the Atlantic and Indian Oceans Unveils Two New Clades for Early Neobatrachian Diversification," *PLoS ONE* 10, no. 11 (November 30, 2015): https://doi.org/10.1371/journal.pone.0143926.
17. Peter S. Cranston, Nate B. Hardy, Geoffrey E. Morse, Louise Puslednik, and Scott R. McCluen, "When Molecules and Morphology Concur: The 'Gondwanan' Midges (Diptera: Chironomidae)," *Systematic Entomology* 35, no. 4 (September 15, 2010): 636–48, https://doi.org/10.1111/j.1365-3113.2010.00531.x.

structures reminiscent of their evolutionary ancestors. For example, many species of snakes have hind limb buds, a remnant of legged ancestors. These hind limb buds quickly degenerate during development. Baleen whales, toothless as adults, have teeth in the early fetal stage. They lose these teeth before birth, but their presence during development is seen as a remnant of their evolutionary relationship with tooth-bearing whales and, more distantly, other mammals.[18]

Common Objections to Evolutionary Theory

Those who believe that evolutionary theory is not compatible with orthodox Christian faith raise several common objections. We have already addressed three of them. We have defined the word *theory* as scientists use it, we have given several examples showing that evolutionary theory is testable, and we have presented numerous examples of the evidence that supports evolutionary theory. Another objection is the claim that evolutionary theory lacks consensus among the scientific community. This is simply not true. The vast majority of scientists not only believe that evolutionary theory is true but see it as the single most important unifying theory in biology and geology.[19] The Pew Research Center surveyed scientists associated

18. Monash University, "Shedding Light on the Origin of the Baleen Whale," ScienceDaily, November 30, 2016, https://tinyurl.com/yaxykub3.
19. Muhammad Aqeel Ashraf and Maliha Sarfraz, "Biology and Evolution of Life Science," *Saudi Journal of Biological Sciences* 23, no. 1 (January 2016): S1–5, https://doi.org/10.1016/j.sjbs.2015.11.012; Jan Sapp, *Evolution by Association: A History of Symbiosis* (New York: Oxford University Press, 1994).

with the American Association of the Advancement of Science (AAAS)—the world's largest multidisciplinary scientific society, started in 1848—and found that 98 percent of them believed that not only did nonhuman life evolve but humans evolved gradually over time.[20] This is an overwhelmingly large percentage.

Some opponents of evolutionary theory argue that evolutionary theory cannot explain the emergence of the first life-form, or that it cannot account for the complexity we see in the diverse life-forms we see today. It is true that scientists cannot fully explain first life, but some of the pieces to this puzzle seem to be filling in. Scientists are able to demonstrate how the primitive chemical building blocks of life might have formed. They can also demonstrate how these building blocks organized into self-replicating assemblies. A puzzling question remained. If nucleic acids encode enzymes and enzymes were necessary for decoding the nucleic acid (replication, transcription, translation), which of these came first? It was a chicken and egg conundrum since, at the time, scientists believed that proteins were the only molecules capable of acting as enzymes to catalyze chemical reactions. Tom Cech, a Nobel Prize-winning scientist at the University of Colorado, studies the process of RNA splicing, in which cellular machinery cuts a segment of noncoding RNA from the larger RNA that was originally transcribed (primary transcript) and seals the two remaining coding segments to produce a functional RNA molecule. Cech's lab, working with RNA from *Tetrahymena thermophila* (a single-

---

20. David Masci, "For Darwin Day, 6 Facts about the Evolution Debate," *Pew Research Center* (blog), February 10, 2017, https://tinyurl.com/y9kjcdu4; Glenn Branch, "Views on Evolution among the Public and Scientists," National Center for Science Education, July 9, 2009, https://tinyurl.com/y9jvjo7u.

celled eukaryote that moves using cilia), demonstrated that *T. thermophila's* rRNA molecule could splice itself—without help from proteins.[21] This rocked the scientific world because here was evidence that nucleic acids, RNA in this case, could function as enzymes. The work put a crack in the chicken-or-egg problem of first life. Since Cech's work, scientists have demonstrated that other RNA molecules can also act as enzymes.[22] The question of how the first lifeform emerged is far from answered, but as evidence begins to create a clearer picture, the gap in our understanding is slowly closing. Christians who argue that evolutionary theory cannot explain the emergence of first life or the level of complexity we see in our world today are often tempted to place God in the gaps of our understanding. This is sometimes called a "God of the gaps" theology, and it is a risky position to hold. If Christians believe in God because of an inability to explain or understand scientific processes, God will shrink as the gaps in our knowledge close.

Newton offers a good example of how a God of the gaps theological argument can fail. Newton did not have a scientific explanation for why all the planets in the solar system move around the sun in the same direction. He placed God in this gap of his understanding by saying,

> The six primary planets are revolved about the sun in circles concentric with the sun, and with motions directed towards the same parts, and almost in the same plane. Ten moons are revolved about the earth, Jupiter, and Saturn, in circles con-

---

21. Kelly Kruger, Paula J. Grabowski, Arthur J. Zaug, Julie Sands, Daniel E. Gottschling, and Thomas R. Cech, "Self-Splicing RNA: Autoexcision and Autocyclization of the Ribosomal RNA Intervening Sequence of Tetrahymena," *Cell* 31, no. 1 (November 1982): 147–57.
22. Peter B. Moore and Thomas A. Steitz, "The Structural Basis of Large Ribosomal Subunit Function," *Annual Review of Biochemistry* 72, no. 1 (2003): 813–50, https://doi.org/10.1146/annurev.biochem.72.110601.135450.

centric with them, with the same direction of motion, and nearly in the planes of the orbits of those planets; but it is not to be conceived that mere mechanical causes could give birth to so many regular motions. . . . This most beautiful system of the sun, planets, and comets, could only proceed from the counsel and dominion of an intelligent and powerful Being.[23]

The gap in Newton's understanding closed when scientists discovered that solar systems form from large clouds of rotating matter. As these rotating clouds collapse under their own gravity, material collects into planets, asteroids, and moons, all rotating around the star in the same direction. If Newton's theology required God to move all the planets of the solar system in the same direction, discovering a natural explanation for this phenomenon diminishes the power of God. Cech's work is a more modern example of the danger of God of the gaps theology. The discovery of catalytic RNA molecules narrows the gap in our understanding of early molecular interactions. If God's necessity is in that gap, God gets smaller with this new scientific knowledge. A better theological position is to remove God from the gaps in our understanding altogether. A better theological position refrains from invoking God to explain the parts of the natural world we cannot so that advances in science have no effect on how necessary or powerful God is.

Some Christians claim that the second law of thermodynamics refutes evolutionary theory. The second law of thermodynamics states that the entropy, or state of disorder, of an isolated system will always increase over time.[24] Evolution is a process in which we see an increase in com-

---

23. Isaac Newton, *The Principia* (Amherst, NY: Prometheus, 2010), General Scholium.
24. Nancy Hall, "Second Law of Thermodynamics," Glenn Research Center at NASA, May 5, 2015, https://tinyurl.com/yam2bdls.

plexity or order over time, which seems to contradict the second law of thermodynamics. Christians who use this argument miss an important requirement of the second law—that it applies to a closed system. Our planet is not a closed system. We continually get energy from the sun. As the sun adds energy in the form of heat and light to our planet, plants build sugars from molecules that are less complex using energy from an external source—the sun. Other organisms use the energy stored in sugar to build complex molecules of their own.

Another common objection to evolutionary theory is that scientists have not observed a new species evolve. One problem scientists have in responding to this objection is that the time required for a new species to evolve is much longer than the lifetime of a scientist. Nevertheless, scientists have been able to observe the evolution of organisms with very short reproductive cycles or have observed changes they would expect in the process of the evolution of a new, more complex species. The Kishony Lab at Harvard Medical School demonstrated the evolution of antibiotic resistance in bacteria, organisms with short reproductive cycles, in a visually stunning video.[25] They were able to watch bacteria evolve from antibiotic-sensitive organisms to organisms that were resistant to one thousand times the effective concentration of antibiotic in only eleven days. In 2016, scientists reported the evolution of two λ phages, viruses that infect bacteria, from a single type.[26] The two new phages used different receptors to infect host

25. "The Evolution of Bacteria on a 'Mega-Plate' Petri Dish (Kishony Lab)," YouTube video, 1:54, uploaded by Harvard Medical School, September 9, 2016, https://tinyurl.com/j9xaqhq.
26. Justin R. Meyer, Devin T. Dobias, Sarah J. Medina, Lisa Servilio, Animesh Gupta, and Richard E. Lenski, "Ecological Speciation of Bacteriophage Lambda in Allopatry and Sympatry," *Science* 354, no. 6317 (December 9, 2016): https://doi.org/10.1126/science.aai8446.

cells. In a twenty-eight-year study, Peter and Rosemary Grant reported finding precisely the changes in finch traits they would expect in the process of speciation when birds were reproductively isolated.[27] Charles R. Brown and Rosemary Bomberger Brown also studied birds. Cliff swallows, *Petrochelidon pyrrhonota*, build cone-shaped nests on the sides of cliffs or under road overpasses and bridges. You can find them during the summer in most of the United States, including western Nebraska, where the two scientists followed bird populations for thirty years. As part of their study, Brown and Brown collected dead swallows. Over the course of their long study, the scientists found fewer birds killed by cars. Changes in traffic patterns could not explain this change. The research team measured the wings of the birds they had collected over the thirty-year study and found that birds killed by cars had longer wings, on average, than those that died in nets (a representation of the general population). Furthermore, the wings of the birds killed by vehicles had lengthened over the course of the study while net-killed swallows had shortened. Brown and Brown proposed that shorter wings enabled birds to dodge traffic more effectively and were therefore less likely to end up as roadkill. Because they avoided fatal collisions with cars, short-winged swallows lived to pass on their shorter-winged genes.[28] A genetic variant (short wings) is not an imperfection in this environment. It is an opportunity. Is this population of swallows evolving? Perhaps. It is far from being a new species. Nevertheless,

27. Peter R. Grant and B. Rosemary Grant, "The Secondary Contact Phase of Allopatric Speciation in Darwin's Finches," *Proceedings of the National Academy of Sciences* 106, no. 48 (December 1, 2009): 20,141, https://doi.org/10.1073/pnas.0911761106.

28. Charles R. Brown and Mary Bomberger Brown, "Where Has All the Road Kill Gone?," *Current Biology* 23, no. 6 (March 18, 2013): R233–34, https://doi.org/10.1016/j.cub.2013.02.023.

studies like these suggest that, given the necessary time, scientists would be able to observe the development of a new species through the process of evolutionary change.

A Better Path

What answer will we have for the Peters of this world—the curious young Christians in our churches interested in science and committed to their faith? How might we respond to those who look to the church to help them find harmony between science and faith? Young earth creationism (YEC) is at odds with the scientific evidence. Suggesting that YEC is the best or only answer risks that young people will follow Peter's path—abandoning their faith when they encounter the evidence for an old earth and evolution. An alternative for the Peters in our churches that embraces both the scientific evidence and takes orthodox Christianity seriously is evolutionary creationism (EC). Evolutionary creationism, sometimes called theistic evolution (TE), is a position held by a number of deeply respected Christians who are scientists.[29] EC embraces cosmological, geological, and biological evidence of an old universe, an old earth, and life emerging through evolutionary processes. EC holds that all of creation, living and nonliving, was created according to a loving, personal Creator's plan and that the emergence of humans bearing God's image was part of that plan from the beginning. This Creator answers prayers and performs miracles—the most important of which was the resurrection of Jesus from the dead. EC points to Colos-

---

29. Francis S. Collins, *The Language of God: A Scientist Presents Evidence for Belief* (London: Simon & Schuster, 2006); Denis O. Lamoureux, *Evolutionary Creation: A Christian Approach to Evolution* (Eugene, OR: Wipf & Stock, 2008); see also BioLogos.org.

sians 1:15–16 as evidence for Jesus's involvement in creation from the beginning. "He is the image of the invisible God, the firstborn of all creation; for in him all things in heaven and on earth were created." And further, this relational God ordains and sustains all the natural processes in the cosmos, physical laws like gravity and biological processes like evolution, for "in him all things hold together" (Col 1:17).

Evolutionary creationism believes that the creation accounts in the early chapters of Genesis are important for revealing God's spiritual truths but are not intended to reveal scientific truths. God created. Creation is very good. Humans bear the image of God, and all humans are sinners in need of grace. EC offers young people a way to hold on to their faith tightly and with thoughtful conviction while embracing their scientific curiosity and participating in science. It teaches them not to fear what they discover. Churches and especially youth programs can participate in helping young people navigate the complicated waters of finding harmony between faith and science. They can start by dispelling any notion that Christians must choose between their faith and what science tells them about evolutionary science.

Let's imagine another Christian young person who has a different experience than the one Peter had. Meet Leah. As a middle-school student, Leah loved science and math. She was encouraged to pursue her interests by her teachers, parents, and youth pastor. As a high-school student, she began to ask questions about how her faith and what she was learning from science fit together. As a child, she understood the stories of creation to be literal, so she was confused and a little distraught. Instead of warning her away from the evils of science and telling her she had to choose faith or evolution, her parents and youth pastor walked with her as they explored different ways of reading Scripture. They read books with her and discussed what she was learning. Her youth pastor invited a scientist who was a trusted member of the church to teach a high-school Sunday-school class about science and faith.[30]

Leah and the other young people of the church practiced asking hard questions and learned that the gospel did not break under the weight of their questions. They discussed the implications of evolutionary theory for their own lives. They concluded that both Scripture and evolutionary theory taught them that they were intimately connected to a good creation that was part of God's grand plan from the beginning. They understood their bodies as temples that were part of God's good creation. In fact, God created their bodies in God's own image. They saw examples in the evolutionary story that imperfections or variations can be opportunities for growth and discussed how that applies to their own bodies and lives.

Leah went to college prepared to hold on to her faith while she encountered hard questions. She majored in science. She was an active member of a Christian group on campus and a local church. She went to graduate school and became a research scientist. She was a respected voice at the table when opportunities arose at her church to discuss science and faith. She was a respected voice at the table when opportunities arose at her university to discuss the moral and responsible use of science in society. Yes, Leah experienced doubts along her faith journey, but she never abandoned her faith. She did not need to. Her church gave her the tools she needed to make room for both science and faith.

---

30. Thea Nyhoff Leunk, *Fossils and Faith: Finding Our Way through the Creation Controversy* (Grand Rapids: Faith Alive Christian Resources, 2005).

2.

Baseball and Barth: Why Youth Ministry Needs Evolution

Jason Lief

> The creation story deals only with the becoming of all things, and therefore with the revelation of God, which is inaccessible to science as such. The theory of evolution deals with that which has become, as it appears to human observation and research and as it invites human interpretation. Thus one's attitude to the creation story and the theory of evolution can take the form of an either/or only if one shuts oneself off completely either from faith in God's revelation or from the mind (or opportunity) for scientific understanding.
> —Karl Barth, *Letters, 1961–1968*

On October 15, 1988, I watched the final innings of game one of the World Series between the Oakland Athletics and the Los Angeles Dodgers. Oakland was the heavy favorite, having won over a hundred games. They had the "bash brothers"—Jose Canseco and Mark McGwire; they had excellent pitching with Dave Stewart, who started that night, and the best closer in baseball—Dennis Eckersley. It was the bottom of the ninth; the Dodgers were down by one run with Eckersley on the mound. After two quick outs, he issued a walk to set up a showdown with Kirk Gibson. Gibson was a great hitter, but he was hurt—a bad knee on one leg and a bad hamstring on the other. He was held out because of injuries, but there he was, hobbling up to the plate to pinch hit in a desperate attempt to make something happen. Two quick strikes found Gibson fighting off pitch after pitch, foul ball after foul ball. He took a couple close pitches, running the count to 3-2. Then Eckersley threw him a high slider. Gibson swung and hit a deep fly ball to right field. Vince Scully, the longtime voice of the Dodgers, called it: "High fly ball into right field, she is gone!" Dodger stadium erupted, Gibson pumped his arms as he hobbled around the bases, and fans stormed the field as he crossed home plate for the game-winning run. The Dodgers went on to win the World Series.

Whenever I talk with students about what it means to get caught up in the human act of play, I show the entire ninth inning of this game. They weren't born when it happened, and most of them don't care about baseball, so it's fun to watch them get caught up in the moment. Because they don't know the outcome, most of them get sucked in, feeling the tension as Gibson fouls off pitch after pitch. Some of them emotionally respond when he hits the home run, getting caught up in the heroics. I show it as a way to talk about what it means to be human, to get caught up in something, to lose ourselves in the moment. I ask them to think about a time when they experienced something similar; it doesn't have to be baseball, just some moment when they felt a part of something bigger. Lately, I'm interested in an entirely different question—what's it like to be Dennis Eckersley? It's one thing to identify with Kirk Gibson—we all dream about it at some point—it's another to identity with Eckersley. The truth? Life is filled with many more Eckersley moments.

One of my favorite conversations to have with middle-school and high-school students is on the topics of imperfection and failure. Failure pushes us to think more deeply about what it means to be human. Most churchgoing kids know the right answers—to be human means being made in the image of God or living to serve and glorify God. When I push it a bit, the discussion usually turns to sin. Evangelical young people know humans are sinful—it's the default response to most questions about the human condition. When I ask them to consider the difference between imperfection and sin, however, they look at me funny. "Is it sinful to miss a jump shot?" I ask. Is it sin that caused Dennis Eckersley to leave a slider up in the strike zone, allowing Gibson to hit it into the stands? Is losing a baseball game sinful? Asking questions about sin and baseball may seem cheesy, but it gets at an important issue—mistaking our humanity with sin. Sometimes Christians have a difficult time differentiating between forms of imperfection, which are basic to living as a human being, and sin, which represents a distortion of our created lives lived before God and our neighbor. So, asking questions about baseball, a game that forces players to make peace with failure, pushes us into important questions about what it means to be human.

Recently, a newspaper article described a reunion between Gibson and Eckersley on the anniversary of the game winning home run:

> Eckersley, 61, said he has long since made his peace with the home run, and not just because he is in the Hall of Fame. He could even appreciate the moment as it happened, he said, for he had found sobriety a couple years earlier. He was grateful to be present, not despondent about the outcome. On a quiet patio outside the ballroom, Eckersley said he would be forever connected to Gibson, and not at all upset about that. As the years pass, he joked, fewer people call him by his given name. "It's like my last name: Hey, Gibson!" Eckersley said. "Every time someone sees me: Hey, Gibson!"[1]

1. Bill Shaikin, "Kirk Gibson and Dennis Eckersley Revisit Classic World Series

Eckersley has "made peace" with what happened because he was "grateful to be present." What would it look like if Christians learned to embrace our mistakes and our failures as an important part of our human experience? What would it look like for youth ministry to help young people live in a way that allows them to say they are grateful to be present? Too often the world young people inhabit, both in the church and in the broader culture, pushes them to hyperspiritualize their identity in the name of some higher ideal. The meaning of life is found in overcoming the limitations of our humanity through never-ending calls for progress and advancement. Put simply, the meaning of human life gets framed as one great big continuous improvement project. Every form of imperfection and failure is deemed unacceptable, as something to be overcome. This leads to an overemphasis on an ideal form of human identity that is unattainable. Unfortunately, the institutions young people inhabit (schools, churches, athletics, etc.) promote the desire to become something they can never become—an ideal form of humanity that isn't real. It's no wonder young people are stressed out and why so many reject the Christianity they're given.

All of this is more problematic when combined with Christian spirituality. The combination of Western capitalism (and its obsession with pragmatic ideals) and Christian spirituality contributes to a new form of hyperspirituality. Moral purity and doctrinal principles turn youth ministry into one more venue for young people to live up to the expectations of adults. It becomes one more place where kids need to improve themselves by accepting Jesus. The end result is the gospel gets separated into the spiritual and material. On the one side you have the so-called spirituality

Moment for a Good Cause," *Los Angeles Times*, April 30, 2016, https://tinyurl.com/jbzlzkz.

found in faith and morality, while on the other are the biological, social, and cultural aspects of embodied life. Too often this split contributes to a view of embodied life as sin. If all of the natural desires, like sexuality, are sinful or impure, then eventually the embodied part of humanity gets lumped in with sin. Which means the purpose of faith, and the hope of Christianity, is to free yourself from the world and the temptations of this embodied life.

The problem this creates has been well documented in the research focusing on young people leaving the church. Christian Smith's work on the faith of adolescents and emergent adults shows how this develops into a form of moralistic therapeutic deism and lack of commitment to orthodox Christianity.[2] Especially for emergent adults, there's a sense that their general understanding of human life is guided by the capitalistic notions of progress. Kenda Dean's *Almost Christian* builds off of Smith's work to show the skewed form of spirituality that emerges when American culture and Christian spirituality are mixed together, making the task of youth ministry much more difficult.[3] As much of the Pew Research suggests, youth ministry can no longer afford to continue down the path of dualistic Christianity. In helping young people come to know the saving work of God in Jesus Christ, we cannot focus solely on getting young people to believe in Jesus or to live moral lives, as important as these are. Youth ministry must help young people answer the question of what it means to live as a human being in this world.

---

2. Christian Smith, *Lost in Transition: The Dark Side of Emerging Adulthood*, ed. with Kari Christoffersen, Hilary Davidson, and Patricia Snell Herzog (New York: Oxford University Press, 2011). Moralistic therapeutic deism is the belief in a God who wants humans to be good and who intervenes in our lives only when we have problems to be solved.
3. Kenda Creasy Dean, *Almost Christian: What the Faith of Our Teenagers Is Telling the American Church* (New York: Oxford University Press, 2010).

Youth ministry cannot afford to perpetuate, either implicitly or explicitly, a dualistic approach to human identity that disconnects the spiritual from the material. This means that congregations and youth programs need to interpret the good news in the context of the embodied lives of young people, addressing their identity as embodied souls, formed not only by the spiritual or the rational but also by the cultural, the biological, and the material. Youth ministry must help young people reclaim their identity from the hyperspirituality that downplays the importance of embodied life, to a Christian understanding of what it means to be a creature made in the image of God, redeemed in Jesus Christ, not for some spiritualized heaven but for creaturely life as part of a renewed creation.

An important part of this is helping young people better understand the difference between sin and imperfection: one is a distortion of the goodness of created life, and one is an aspect of what it means to live as a human creature. To go further, youth ministry needs to cultivate practices that help young people embrace the goodness of embodied life by changing the narrative on such topics as sexuality, gender, work, and play. It means having important conversations about death and suffering, what it means to live in relationships with others, and how culture and faith are connected. We need to affirm that Christ is Lord of embodied human life, over every creature and biological processes. We need to affirm that Christ is Lord over our cultural lives just as much as our spiritual lives. This is the biblical and theological task of youth ministry.

This is why youth ministry must engage in a positive dialogue with evolutionary theory. For too long the negative response of evangelicals to Darwin's theory of evolution has contributed to a dualistic approach to human identity. Because we're too afraid to explore the positive contributions of these theories, we insist on giving young people safe interpretations of the Bible that lead to safe beliefs. The result is an unnecessary tension between science and Christianity. As Christian young people are exposed to the findings of scientific research in colleges and universities (or on PBS), some feel they are forced to choose between the Christian faith they grew up with and the scientific worldview they have discovered. This is a false dichotomy and a false choice. Christians do not have to choose between faith and science, and they certainly don't have to turn to turn to alternative, anti-evolutionary forms of Christian science to bring the two together. The word God speaks in Jesus Christ is just as much at the center of scientific exploration as it is at the center of a Sunday night youth event. Our task, as the Christian community, as leaders in the church, as leaders, pastors, and teachers in the field of youth ministry, is to help young people encounter this theological truth.

Too often, the relationship between science and faith focuses on how to read Genesis, which leads to a discussion of the methods we use to interpret the Bible, as well as different philosophical and scientific approaches to truth. At the heart of this discussion is the nature of language, how words and concepts make reality present to us, and whether the creation accounts in Genesis should be read as history or science. Jesus comes into the discussion in relation to the question of whether Adam and Eve were real, historical people. This is where the faith and science discussion turns into a salvation issue. After all, why would Jesus have to die if there was no historical Adam or historical fall? While this discussion is important, it usually remains stuck in the realm of hermeneutics, history, and truth. Only tangentially does it address the person of Christ.

Focusing too much on Genesis runs the risk of diminishing the importance of embodied life and scientific inquiry in two ways: The first is when Christians argue for an interpretation of Genesis that tries to reconcile evolutionary theory with the Bible. Usually, this involves arguments about the Hebrew word for *day* or God's perspective of time (you know, a day is like a thousand years). This is a problem because it disconnects the gospel from creation. When Genesis is seen as poetics, mythical writing, or theological writing (which it is), it doesn't have anything to do with science. As a result, science and faith run parallel to each other, not having any connection other than a doctrine of creation that believes God is the first cause. But this isn't Christianity—it's closer to Deism. The other approach interprets Genesis as strict, literal history and science. While this avoids Deism, it damages the way we read the Bible, not to mention it dismisses most of the findings of contemporary science. The first leaves theology and science intact but never intersecting while the second collapses science into biblical theology, which does damage to both science and theology.

The problem with these approaches is that creation is reduced to the context for the more important stuff—the spiritual salvation of humanity in the work of Jesus Christ. Don't get me wrong, the saving work of Christ is central to Christian faith, so I am in no way saying Christians shouldn't focus on Christ's work. What I object to is the idea that creation is just context; I'm questioning the disconnection that results between Christ and creation. As we will see in the work of Dietrich Bonhoeffer and Karl Barth, if Christ is at the center of creation, then faith and science cannot be disconnected, nor can theology reduce the Bible to scientific propositions. The point is that creation is not secondary; creation is not merely context for the more important stuff—creation exists in covenantal relationship with God.

The theology of twentieth-century Swiss theologian Karl Barth provides a different way of framing the relationship between science and youth ministry. Instead of starting with Genesis, we begin with the incarnation, specifically the question, Why did God become human? This opens up other important questions: What is the nature of sin in relation to our humanity? How do we make sense of the incarnation in the context of salvation? By exploring Barth's answers to these questions, youth ministry, as practical theology, has an opportunity to move beyond arguments about Genesis and engage with science on the topic of human identity. By framing the issue this way, it's possible to explore the positive contributions that evolutionary theory has to offer theology. More specifically, it allows us to explore how the incarnation illuminates what can be known about human life through evolutionary theory, helping us better understand what it means to be human—made in the image of the crucified and risen Christ. To demonstrate this, I will explore the theological ideas of Karl Barth and Franciscan theologian Ilia Delio, focusing on the incarnation as the revelation of God's identity and God's saving action.

Karl Barth Likes Creation

Some scholars think Karl Barth doesn't like creation. He has the reputation of opposing anything that vaguely smells like general or natural revelation because he's opposed to the idea that we can start with the created world and get to the God revealed in the Bible. A closer look, however, shows a more nuanced approach. Barth's problem with the special/general revelation distinction is it disconnects the revelation of God's saving action in Jesus Christ from God's identity as the Creator. Jesus Christ is, for Barth, the Word of God spoken before the foundations of the world. As Paul says in Ephesians, God "chose us in Christ before the foundation of the world to be holy and blameless before him in love" (Eph 1:4). Paul says something similar in Colossians, where he writes, "He is the image of the invisible God, the firstborn of all creation; for in him all things in heaven and on earth were created, things visible and invisible" (Col 1:15–16). Based on passages like this, Barth believes it is impossible to talk about creation without also talking about Jesus Christ. Christ and creation cannot be separated. Natural or general revelation that separates Christ from culture and creation always ends in idolatry, or the worship of a god who is not God.

For Barth, creation must always be connected with the incarnation of Jesus Christ. This means that Barth refuses to see creation as an event separate from God's saving work in the history of Israel and Jesus Christ. Because everything God does it connected to Jesus Christ, the act of creation derives its meaning from what Barth refers to as its "inner beginning, its eternal source in God's decision and plan."[4] The creation itself, including the creation of human beings, is grounded in the grace and love of God revealed in the word spoken before the foundations of the cosmos.

Everything God does flows out of the love between the Father, Son, and Holy Spirit, which means that both creation and salvation are grounded in love. The meaning of creation is to exist in relationship with God. For Barth, creation is an expression of incarnational love, as "the Son of Man, the word made flesh—is the true and genuine basis of

---

4. Karl Barth, *Church Dogmatics*, III/1 (London: T&T Clark, 2004), 43. *Church Dogmatics* hereafter cited as *CD*.

creation."[5] For Barth, the creation is born out of the love of the Father for the Son. But this is not the Son (the second person of the Trinity) without incarnation; for Barth, this love is the love for the Son who becomes incarnate from all eternity, which means that "God loved man and man's whole world from all eternity, even before it was created, and in and in spite of its absolute lowliness and non-holiness, indeed its anti-godliness."[6]

The problem with other approaches to the relationship between science and faith is that they tend to disconnect creation from the incarnation of Jesus Christ, reading the creation stories as a prefall covenant of works that are separate from salvation history. The fall, in this context, makes another form of covenant—a covenant of grace—necessary as a response to sin. This is the basis for the general/special revelation split, which leads to a hard split between creaturely forms of life (bodies, animals, tiny little rocks) and the spiritual life that relates to faith in Christ. For Barth, however, creation cannot be separated from the revelation of God in Jesus Christ precisely because "God wills and God creates the creature for the sake of His Son or Word."[7] Creation is not separate from the history of salvation, it is a necessary part of this history. God's love revealed in the incarnation of the Son in Jesus Christ is, for Barth, the center and meaning of history, which means it is also the center and meaning of creation. Barth writes, "That we can understand our creaturely existence as such as the gift of divine grace depend—if 'grace' is not to be just a pious word—on the fact that its creation and preservation is a concrete act of God and therefore a historical reality fulfilling time. Then and only then does our crea-

---

5. Barth, *CD* III/1, 51.
6. Barth, *CD*, III/1, 50.
7. Barth, *CD* III/1, 59.

turely existence as such already stand in connection with the organizing center of all God's acts, with the reality of Jesus Christ; then and only then can we believe in our existence and nature as we believe in Jesus Christ, as be believe in the triune God."[8]

You might be asking: Who cares? How is this not just one more abstract theological argument that makes things more complex than they have to be? This matters because when the incarnation is understood as God's response to human sin, the material creation becomes separated from grace and salvation. Sure, we need to take care of creation, God called it good, we have physical bodies, and we like to go hiking, but what really matters is the spiritual side of things. This shows itself when people bring up the "salvation issue" response. You know, the "It's fine that you all argue about these things, but it's not a salvation issue." What they mean is, "What really matters is whether a person is saved, so that when they die they will go to some spiritual heaven." They will admit that our bodies are temples, but what is most important about our humanity is our soul, our spirit—the spiritual me that will one day leave the body and go to heaven. The body, in this context, is a container for what really matters.

For Barth, creation is an act of love and grace that derives its meaning from the incarnation of the Son. Creation is not just context—it is not a secondary act that sets the stage for the more important acts; it is an expression of God's love and grace. This means the material creation is inseparable from the spiritual; there is no divide between the two. Human beings are embodied souls, which means our material stuff matters. How we think about this matters because it has important consequences for how we think

---

8. Barth, *CD* III/1, 61.

about science and faith. For Barth, it goes much further, affecting the way we think about salvation.

Plan A or Plan B?

In Barth's theology, Jesus Christ is the primary lens for interpreting the creation. This means that the incarnation is not just a response to human sin, it is an expression of love and grace from which God creates. In Jesus Christ creation is "predestined to participate in the history which has its ground and direction in the will of God."[9] This means God's relationship with creation is established as a covenant of grace from before the foundation of the world in the election of Jesus Christ. According to Barth, this "forbids us to think meanly of Jesus Christ, His kingdom and His church, as if the work of our salvation and redemption were a kind of afterthought which we might ignore in view of creation as God's first and principal work. It is precisely in view of creation that we cannot possibly ignore Jesus Christ."[10]

Put simply, the incarnation is not plan B. It is not a response to human sin; it is, instead, the outworking of God's eternal decision to be for creation in the election of Jesus Christ. Barth writes, "If by the Son or the Word of God we understand concretely Jesus, the Christ, and therefore very God and very man, as he existed in the counsel of God from all eternity and before creation, we can see how far it was not only appropriate and worthy but necessary that God should be the Creator."[11] It was necessary because the act of creation flows from the will of the triune God

9. Barth, *CD* III/1, 46.
10. Barth, *CD* III/1, 46.
11. Barth, *CD* III/1, 51.

expressed in the love of the Father for the incarnate Son. Barth writes, "The fact that God has regard to His Son—the Son of Man, the Word made flesh—is the true and genuine basis of creation. To be sure there was no other necessity than that of His own free love."[12]

This is important because it places the incarnation at the center of God's creative action. Instead of a rescue mission, the incarnation reveals God's purpose for creation from the very beginning. It affirms the time-bound, material creation as God's intention for all living creatures. Barth writes, "But if God's creation is a history, this means that it takes place in time. Time, in contradistinction to eternity, is the form of existence of the creature."[13] To be a creature, for Barth, is to exist in time as an object of God's love. To be a creature, for Barth, is "to be on the way," and the only way for God and creation to have relationship is by God's "condescension to it, by His entrance into its form of existence."[14]

An important theme in Barth's *Church Dogmatics* is what he refers to as the Yes and No of God. He says that "God the Creator did not say No, nor Yes and No, but Yes to what He created."[15] He goes on to say that the creation, as the bringing forth of a time-bound, material world, "is not rejection, but election and acceptance."[16] Barth doesn't allow Christians any other way to think about creation—it is good, and it is affirmed by God. This affirmation means that creation is "elected and not rejected, it is the object of God's good pleasure."[17] Jesus Christ reveals God's lov-

---

12. Barth, *CD* III/1, 51.
13. Barth, *CD* III/1, 67.
14. Barth, *CD* III/1, 69.
15. Barth, *CD* III/1, 330.
16. Barth, *CD* III/1, 331.
17. Barth, *CD* III/1, 366.

ing Yes for all of creation. The material stuff of creation is not just a temporary stop on the way to a spiritual heaven; God loves material stuff, including human bodies. Humans were never meant to be perfect if perfection means some abstract form of hyperspirituality. More importantly, we should never confuse sin with limits of material creation. When this happens, individuals and communities see their embodied existence as something to be overcome or conquered. For young people especially, there is a temptation to mistake spirituality with abstraction, to chase after some ideal identity that leaves embodied life behind. Of course, sin is real and it is pervasive, but total depravity does not mean every single aspect of our humanity is totally evil. Sin is a distortion of God's good creation that has terrible consequences, which brings us to Barth's view of what it means to be saved in the death and resurrection of Jesus Christ.

Jesus Saves

The question "Why did God become human?" has many different theological answers. The default answer in contemporary Christianity is that God became human in Jesus Christ because Adam and Eve sinned (the fall), which meant that God had to come save us. The most influential explanations of how this works, in Western Christianity anyway, are Anselm's "satisfaction theory" and the Protestant version known as the "penal theory" of the atonement. Anselm's basic idea is that when humans sinned, they robbed God of something (honor or obedience). In the process, they offended God's holiness and justice. As a result of this offense, God must punish sin so God's anger and wrath at the offense can be appeased. This can happen through the offering of a gift, called "propitiation," but this gift must go "above and beyond." Like when a partner is unfaithful, it does no good to say "Okay, I won't do it again." The offending party needs to prove it by going above and beyond what is already owed—either by offering a gift or demonstrating their love in significant ways. Or, in the case of the penal theory, someone must pay the penalty for sin because God's wrath has to be satisfied. Because humans did the crime, a human being must either offer propitiation or pay the penalty. The problem? What more can we give God than our own life? But we already owe God our whole life, which puts us in a quandary. Humans did the crime, so humans must make it right. The problem, however, is there's nothing we can give God that goes "above and beyond."

In the incarnation, God comes to do what humans can't. In Jesus Christ, God becomes a human being to deal with sin. Jesus, the perfect human, doesn't have to die, but he offers his life as a "gift"—going above and beyond—to appease God's wrath and restore honor. Or, Jesus dies, taking upon himself the punishment due because of sin, which appeases God's justice. This view of the incarnation focuses on what God came to do—save us from sin and the wrath, punishment, and judgment that is the result. For Anselm, the incarnation is primarily instrumental—God becomes human not because God intended to from the beginning but because God needed to take on human nature to make satisfaction for sin. Grounded in a medieval form of economics based upon honor and gift exchange, God became human to make satisfaction for sin, with the sacrifice of Christ as the gift that satisfies God's wrath, making reconciliation between humanity and God possible. For the Protestant Reformers, the incarnation is the means by which God satisfies God's justice on our behalf, taking the punishment for human sin on the cross so that those who believe in Jesus Christ can be declared righteous—justified by faith in the saving work of Jesus Christ.

Both the satisfaction and penal theories of the atonement see the incarnation as a response to sin. Both interpret the death and resurrection of Jesus Christ as a sacrifice that appeases God's wrath, making reconciliation with God possible. Beyond some of the philosophical questions this raises (Why does God have to save humanity from God?), an important question to consider about this view of the atonement is whether it contributes to a diminished view of our humanity. I am not suggesting that everyone who holds this view has a negative view of their humanity, nor am I suggesting every part of this approach should be rejected. There are aspects of the satisfaction and penal theories that are biblical. I am concerned that they unintentionally abstract human identity by making the boundary between sin (fallen humanity) and humanity (our good embodied existence) fuzzy. If God becomes human in Jesus Christ to save us from sin, and if we equate being human with being sinful, it makes sense that some might see God's work of salvation in Jesus Christ as freeing us from our humanity. Admittedly, this is a distortion of Christianity, but a distortion that's more likely in a culture that abstracts human identity in many other ways.

What if the incarnation is not, primarily, a response to human sin? What if the incarnation was God's intention all along? There have been theologians as far back as Irenaeus in the second century who made this argument. I'm not interested in talking about whether the incarnation would have happened if the fall had not happened—that's just speculation. The fall did happen, and sin is very real. However, Barth's theology provides a way of talking about the incarnation not as plan B, not as a response to sin, but as

God's purpose and intent from "before the foundations of the earth." He frames the incarnation as the basis for creation and the foundation for God's gracious covenant with humanity from the very beginning. The atonement does not need its own special covenant; it is already possible because of God's decision to be for creation before the foundations of the world. This means that the work of reconciliation is already present in the election of Jesus Christ where God says yes to the creation, thus deciding to be for the creation. Barth writes,

> God Himself lives and acts and speaks and suffers and triumphs for all men as this one man. When this takes place, atonement takes place. But the final thing which takes place here—just as it cannot be something provisional—cannot be a second or later thing. It can only reveal the first thing. What takes place here is the accomplishment and therefore the revelation of the original and basic will of God, as a result of which all the other works and words of God take place.[18]

He also writes, "The work of atonement in Jesus Christ is the fulfillment of the communion of Himself with man and of man with Himself which he willed and created at the very first. Even in the face of man's transgression He cannot allow it to be destroyed. He does not permit that which He willed as Creator—the inner meaning and purpose and basis of the creation—should be perverted or arrested by the transgression of man."[19] The incarnation, historically speaking, seems to be a response to sin; but for Barth, the incarnation is an event that is already "determined from the very first and already initiated."[20] He writes, "Even in this particular form it is the accomplishment of his covenant

---

18. Barth, *CD* IV/1, 35–36.
19. Barth, *CD* IV/1, 36.
20. Barth, *CD* IV/1, 36.

will. Even more, it is the affirmation and consumption of the institution of the covenant between Himself and man which took place in and with the creation."[21]

Seeing the incarnation as the fulfillment of God's will for creation speaks to God's purpose for humanity—to live as creatures in covenantal relationship with God. This means that God's saving action in Jesus Christ does not take us away from embodied life into some perfected, idealized existence. The reality of human sin, while pervasive, does not mean every part of our humanity is totally evil. On the contrary, Barth interprets the work of God in the incarnation of Jesus Christ as the fulfillment of what it means to live as creatures in this world. The reconciliation that occurs in the death and resurrection of Jesus Christ is the restoration of our humanity as God's convent partner and the affirmation of creation within the divine life of the Trinity.

What does this mean for youth ministry? The good news for young people is that God is not saving them from their humanity; in Jesus Christ God calls young people to finally live as the human beings God calls them to be. This theological understanding allows for a holistic approach to youth ministry. While young people need to hear the saving power of the gospel, the purpose is not to call them to some higher spiritual existence apart from embodied life. Instead, it is for the purpose of young people being reconciled to their embodied life in Jesus Christ. In Jesus, God reveals to young people God's desire is for them to live as human beings, redeemed and forgiven, taking on the new humanity of Christ so they can live as God's people in the world. This means that a central task of youth ministry is to help young people embrace their humanity in Jesus Christ. This approach opens youth ministry to new possibilities.

21. Barth, *CD* IV/1, 36.

Sure, there will still be teaching and worship, lock ins, concerts, and pizza, but there will also be a focus on justice and politics, economics and poverty. Youth ministry will also emphasize our relationship to the creation, the goodness of cultural life and work, and a positive approach to sexuality, friendships, and family relationships. Camp programs will help young people embrace their embodied experience as they reconnect with the creation, and youth pastors will help young people engage environmental issues as well as questions about the relationship between new forms of technology and our humanity.

This is nothing new—many youth groups and churches already address these issues. However, Barth's view of the incarnation opens up the possibility for youth ministry to engage these issues from a theological perspective. Doing so provides a way for the Christian community to minister to young people by taking on the anxieties and fears that are directly related to the abstractions of contemporary Western culture and the spiritualized abstractions present within evangelical forms of Christianity. At the same time, youth pastors will find their work is grounded in the revelation of God's will for young people in Jesus Christ, as they help young people live into their humanity revealed in the incarnation.

Karl Barth, the Scientist

An important way for youth ministry to help young people live into their humanity is through a positive conversation with science. Traditionally, youth ministry has seen this as outside of their area, except for possibly preparing young people to withstand the atheistic science they might encounter from liberal college professors. Unfortunately, this contributes to the dualism that sees material life in conflict with Christian faith. This is unacceptable for Barth because Jesus Christ is always at the center of created life. In book 3 of the *Dogmatics*, Barth discusses the place of scientific study in the life of the Christian community. He talks about how human beings are deeply connected to the earth, and that if we forget to "remain loyal to the earth" we will never understand what it means to be fully human.[22] To understand our humanity in relation to the created world is an important part of the theological task, one that takes place through interdisciplinary dialogue. For Barth, the fact that Jesus is fully human gives meaning to other disciplines, opening the door to a theological conversation with the sciences.

Barth insists that the sciences must not be held captive to theology. Because we lack absolute certainty in the sciences, Barth argues Christians are free to move from "one world-view to another without being untrue to itself, i.e. its object. It is always free in relation to all such conceptions."[23] Like Augustine before him, Barth does not want the Bible or theology to become trapped in a particular metaphysical or scientific way of seeing the world. Instead, we are free to respond to new insights and new theories that help us better understand the way creation works. This also helps us understand Barth's opposition to natural theology as faith guards against making any worldview absolute. The Word of God revealed in Jesus Christ does not speak to the nature of the cosmos.[24] This Word does, however, reveal the relational or covenantal nature of the human person as a creature living in relationship with God. The Bible does not address the inner workings of the cosmos,

22. Barth, *CD* III/2, 4.
23. Barth, *CD* III/2, 8.
24. Barth, *CD* III/2, 11.

nor does it tell us everything about God's relationship with other parts of the creation. Barth writes, "The cosmos is not without man. . . . But this does not mean that we can go on to assert that . . . the cosmos could not exist over and above its special relation to man, in quite other dimensions and in quite another sense. But we do not know these other dimensions or this other sense in the cosmos. We know the cosmos only through its relation to man. Yet, this does not justify us in supposing that its life is necessarily exhausted in this relation."[25]

Barth wants us to know that an important part of being fully human is to be part of the cosmos. He even refers to humans as being "earthly" in both body and soul, and that heaven is not our real home. Heaven is, according to Barth, "the sphere from which God speaks and acts towards man. Hence it is not a sphere to which man belongs by nature, not even in virtue of his soul. For in the language of the Bible the soul is simply the earthly life of man, and not at all a divine or heavenly component of being."[26] Barth is very clear that the material cosmos "determines" what it means to be human, forming and shaping our life as embodied creatures.

Barth criticizes both science and theology when they try to name and understand God. When this happens, Barth makes the radical claim that Christians must become good atheists, rejecting the god that is not the God revealed in Jesus Christ. At the same time, he believes that when science does not overstep its boundaries, scientific exploration cannot be called an "unspiritual work."[27] He writes, "To the extent that it remains within its limits, and does not attempt to be more or less than exact science, it is a good

---

25. Barth, *CD* III/2, 15.
26. Barth, *CD* III/2, 16.
27. Barth, *CD* III/2, 25.

work; as good as man himself as God created him."[28] Theology that takes seriously the revelation of God in Jesus Christ allows and encourages the Christian community to engage in scientific exploration. Not dogmatically, which is true of some who promote evolutionary theory, but in humility, generosity, and integrity, seeking to understand the world in which humans live and the relationship of human identity to the created world.

This is where Barth provides an important way forward in the relationship between faith and science. When Christ is recognized as the center of created life, the Christian community is free to explore the creation in the light of evolutionary theory and scientific discovery. When undertaken in humility, evolutionary theory is not a threat to faith; instead, it allows for a deepening of faith through understanding. When evolutionary theory is framed as a paradigm for understanding the human person in the light of Jesus Christ, we are free to follow the scientific evidence where it leads. The importance of this freedom is the recognition that evolutionary theory opens up the possibility of a certain type of world and a particular way in which human beings inhabit this world. It pushes us to think about our embodiment, our particular human identity, as it is deeply interconnected with the created world and about a new type of embodied spirituality that is opened up to suffering and death in new ways. This way of thinking about evolutionary theory in relation to Jesus Christ provides new ways of thinking about the creation, about the nature of sin, about human finitude, and about the power of death and resurrection. The beautiful thing about Barth's theology is it provides the freedom for Christians to go down this path in faith, without fear, knowing that scientific inquiry cannot

---

28. Barth, *CD* III/2, 25.

disprove the revelation of God's love for the world in Jesus Christ.

Conclusion: What Are We Saved For?

If youth ministry is going to live into its task of proclaiming the gospel, it must address the lived experience of young people. A dualistic approach that makes a hard separation between the spiritual and the material does not help young people live into their identity as human creatures. Too often evangelical Christianity approaches salvation as though we are being saved *from* something, which means we end up engaging in culture wars over issues pertaining to science or sexuality or social media. An unintended consequence of this is that a wedge is driven between the embodied existence of young people and what they perceive to be Christian faith. Barth's theology offers a different way of thinking about God's action in Jesus Christ. Rather than emphasize human beings are saved *from* something, Barth shows us that Christianity proclaims we are being saved *for* something. In Jesus Christ we are called to become fully human, to live into our identity as God's creatures. Yes, we must take sin seriously, but Barth refuses to give sin more than it's due. Instead, he believes the Christian community must focus on God's Yes, on how God is fulfilling God's purpose for creation spoken in the beginning in the incarnation, death, and resurrection of Jesus Christ.

This message has important consequences. In Christ we receive the revelation of God's love for creation, humanity, and all creatures. We affirm our embodied life and the relationships this includes. We see culture not as something on the periphery of the Christian life but as a fundamental part of our human identity. The incarnation is the divine affirmation of our humanity, the embrace of our finitude and particularity, and the embrace of our condition of becoming. This perspective opens up the possibility that the Christian community can embrace created life in the context of Christ's death and resurrection, knowing that God is not saving us from our humanity but is at work giving our humanity back to us. This is certainly good news for young people living in the West. Burdened with abstraction, with competition, with ideal visions of the good life, many of them struggle beneath the weight of unattainable expectations. What youth ministry in the key of Barth offers is freedom from the idolatry of perfection and ideals, and the revelation of God's love for finite humanity. Which brings me back to baseball.

For the past few years, I have coached junior-high baseball. My son is on the team, giving me a window into the angst of junior-high boys. There's an anxiety, a fear, that grips many of them—an intense fear of failure combined with a fear of looking silly or making mistakes. So, they play tentative, they play scared, which is always counterproductive. After one game during which my son made errors and struck out multiple times, he was frustrated, mad, and had tears in his eyes during the drive home. So, we talked it over. I told him that baseball is a sport that forces you to deal with failure. You can't be perfect, so you have to be willing to put yourself out there, step up to the plate, strike out, and then be ready to do it all again. The walk back to the dugout after a strikeout is a lonely one, as is waiting between pitches after dropping a fly ball or making a throwing error. I told my son, "You have to be able to deal with failure, or you can't play the game and enjoy it. Baseball is a sport where someone fails two out of three times and makes it to the Hall of Fame. Failure is a part of the game. It's what makes it hard, but it's also what makes it beautiful." This is the truth that Dennis Eckersley understood when he was able to be fully present while giving up the game-winning home run. This is what Karl Barth invites us to consider as we think about the incarnation not as a response to sin but as God's embrace of our humanity. This is the task of youth ministry—to help young people live into their humanity in Christ, to no longer be afraid, and to embrace the beauty of their finite lives lived before the face of God. This, I believe, is the importance of helping young people engage the important scientific questions, not out of fear but out of love for their embodied human life.

3.

Adam and Lucy: What Evolution Says about Being Human

Sara Sybesma Tolsma

> We're all of us guinea pigs in the laboratory of God. Humanity is just a work in progress.
> —Tennessee Williams, *Camino Real*[1]

From Monkeys?

Many Christians accept that the earth is old. Many even accept that living organisms came to be through the natural process of evolution. However, they often recoil at the notion that humans also evolved. It raises many questions: From what species did humans evolve? Does it diminish the special place humans believe they hold in the natural world? What about the image of God? As interesting as these questions are, they're not questions you bring up around the family dinner table. I was quite surprised, therefore, to arrive at a recent family reunion and learn that my mother had been telling family members that I was cowriting a book. They immediately peppered me with questions. Who's the other author? Who will publish it? Is this a requirement for your job? Finally they asked the dreaded

---

1. Susan Ratcliffe, *Oxford Treasury of Sayings and Quotations* (Oxford: Oxford University Press, 2011), 216.

question: What is the book about? I said the book was about science and youth ministry and, since I'm the scientist, I'm responsible for writing about evolution. My cousin asked if I was writing about microevolution or macroevolution. When I said "both," he stated that there's no evidence for macroevolution. So, we had a conversation about whales. Later, my aunt cornered me and asked, "Evolution? You mean like humans came from monkeys?" Her tone let me know that what I was proposing was distasteful. I explained that sharing a common ancestor was different from "coming from monkeys."

Discussing human evolution pushes buttons and generates passionate responses. In the Christian community, an evolutionary understanding of human origins raises (legitimate) questions about the historicity of Adam and Eve, the fall, and the role of Christ's redemptive work. It's important that we don't avoid these issues but explore the connections between human evolution and faith. Connecting our faith with human evolution raises important questions: What does evolution have to say about human relationships, our relationships with nonhuman creatures and the rest of the earth, and our relationship with God? Why is it so difficult to see our physical bodies, our creatureliness, as part of Barth's "on the way"?[2] Before we tackle the implications of human evolution, however, we need to examine the evidence that supports the story of human evolution.

---

2. Karl Barth, *The Work of Creation*, part 1 of *The Doctrine of Creation*, vol. 3 of *Church Dogmatics* (New York: Continuum, 2004), 69.

Human Evolution: An Analogy from Language

The fact that scientists look backward in time to understand the evolutionary relationships between humans and the rest of creation is difficult to grasp. We know that fossils are part of the picture, but fossils are rare and sometimes give the mistaken impression that evolution works in large, clearly distinguishable steps—that one species becomes a different one instantaneously. Evolution does not work this way for humans or any other species. Instead, it works through incremental changes over a long time.

In *Adam and the Genome*, Dennis Venema uses the evolution of language as a way to understand human evolution.[3] He specifically focuses on the development of modern English from Anglo-Saxon English. He begins with a Scripture passage familiar to most Christians, John 14:6, from the earliest known English Gospel, *Da Haglan Godspel on Englisc*, written around 990 in Anglo-Saxon English (Figure 3.1).[4] Venema follows the evolution of this familiar Scripture verse, looking at the record left for us in the Wycliffe Bible from 1395, the Tyndale Bible from 1525, the King James Version from 1611, the Cambridge edition of the King James Bible from 1769, and finally in modern translations.[5] Over time, the spelling and grammar change from a nearly unrecognizable form

---

3. Dennis R. Venema and Scot McKnight, *Adam and the Genome: Reading Scripture after Genetic Science* (Grand Rapids: Brazos, 2017), 19–42.
4. Benjamin Thorpe, ed., *Da Halgan Godspel on Englisc* (London: Richard & John E. Taylor, 1842), https://tinyurl.com/ybbetdxt.
5. "Parallel Viewing: John 14:1," The Bible Tool, https://tinyurl.com/y7l9779f; "The Tyndale New Testament 1526," Original Bibles, July 26, 2014, https://tinyurl.com/ybpwm6kn; "The Gospel according to S. John. Chapter 14," King James Bible Online, https://tinyurl.com/y7bre8rd; "Gospel

in 990 (Figure 3.1[6]) to versions that are more recognizable in modern versions. Venema makes the point that, although language changes incrementally over time, we see only a few examples of those changes when we look back from our vantage point.

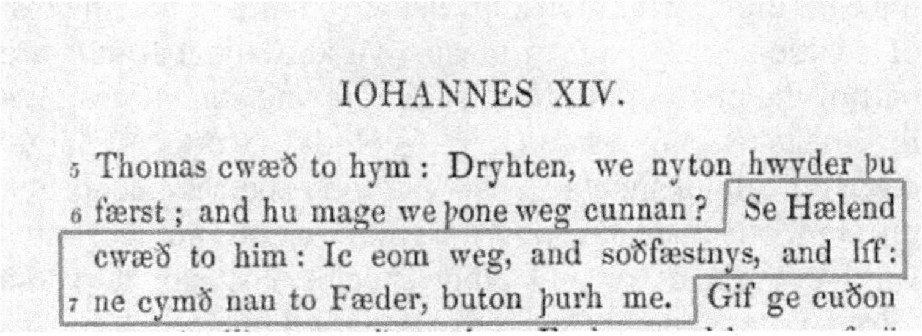

IOHANNES XIV.

5 Thomas cwæð to hym : Dryhten, we nyton hwyder þu
6 færst ; and hu mage we þone weg cunnan ? Se Hælend
cwæð to him : Ic eom weg, and soðfæstnys, and líf :
7 ne cymð nan to Fæder, buton þurh me. Gif ge cuðon

Figure 3.1. John 14:6 (outlined) from Da Haglan Godspel on Englisc.

Michael Kensak, my colleague in the English department, studies old texts. He is familiar with the ways words and word use change over time. His eyes lit up when I told him I had just looked up *Da Haglan Godspel on Englisc*, and he provided another example. The Lord's Prayer (Matt 6:9–13) is familiar to most of us. Like John 14:6, the English words for the Lord's Prayer have changed over time (Figure 3.2). We have snapshots of the gradual change in surviving books. The dramatic differences we see in the four versions spanning one thousand years did not happen abruptly. The changes in spelling and grammar were gradual. Books are remnants that represent snapshots of gradual changes in language. Similarly, fossils are remnants of gradual anatomical changes in organisms.

according to John," Christian Library, https://tinyurl.com/ycu9tqkd; Venema and McKnight, *Adam and the Genome*.
6. Thorpe, *Da Halgan Godspel on Englisc*, 220.

Old English 10th Century	Middle English 14th Century	Early Modern English 17th Century	Late Modern English 20th Century
urn gedæghwamlican hlaf syle us todæg and forgyf us ure gyltas swa swa we forgyfað urum gyltendum	gyue to us this dai oure breed and forgyue to us oure dettis as we forgyuen to oure dettouris	Give vs this day our daily bread. And forgiue vs our debts, as we forgiue our debters.	Give us this day our daily bread. And forgive us our debts, as we also have forgiven our debtors.
Exeter Book c. 975	Wycliffe c. 1380	KJV 1611	NRSV, 1989

Figure 3.2. Two sentences from the Lord's Prayer as it transitioned over a thousand years.

Spelling also changes over time, as illustrated by Dennis Venema, who describes changes in the spelling of *truth* from Anglo-Saxon to Modern English. Within a single population, we see an evolution of one word "progressively between very similar forms: treuthe, truthe, trueth, and finally the modern truth."[7] Venema points out that none of these changes were instantaneous. They were gradual changes in preference with two variants coexisting until the correctness of one won out over the other. Similarly, we can examine a word from the Lord's Prayer over time (Figure 3.2). The word we use to describe granting pardon

---

7. Venema and McKnight, *Adam and the Genome*, 21.

is spelled four different ways in the four English versions of the Lord's prayer: forgyf, forgyue, forgiue, and forgive. These changes did not occur as dramatic shifts in spelling. Rather, we might imagine that yf became yue, with both used for a time but yue considered correct by the time the Wycliffe Bible was printed in 1380. Language, like species, is on the way in a slow, gradual process of continual change.

Considering how language changes over time can help us understand how evolution works. Language changes slowly over time, but we do not see those changes fluidly when we look backward. We infer fluid changes from the remnants that have been left behind for us. Alternate spellings and words are analogous to genetic variants that biologists call alleles. Genetics and the tools it brings have been revolutionary in helping scientists understand the process of evolution and unpack evolutionary relationships between modern organisms and our ancient ancestors.

Genetics 101

Some of the best evidence for human evolution comes from genetic studies. The Human Genome Project stimulated the development of rapid, inexpensive sequencing technologies, often referred to as next generation sequencing (NGS). NGS technologies have reduced the cost of sequencing a genome from approximately $100 million in 2001 to $1,000 in 2016.[8] Inexpensive sequencing means that scientists have sequenced many genomes. The National Center for Biotechnology Information (NCBI)

---

8. Kris Wetterstrand, "DNA Sequencing Costs: Data," National Human Genome Research Institute, https://tinyurl.com/y8bgfou3.

lists more than 3,500 genomes sequenced to date.[9] The list includes humans, apes, whales, zebra fish, horses, mice, fruit flies, mosquitoes, worms, corn, wheat, and multitudes of bacteria and viruses. Scientists have an abundance of data with which to work.

In order to understand genetic evidence for common ancestry, we need to pause for a brief genetics lesson. The heritable instructions for making us unique individuals, our genetic blue print, are contained in a large biomolecule called DNA. DNA is a long molecule made up of repeating units that come in four types. The units are called nucleotides, and the four types of nucleotides are adenine, cytosine, guanine, and thymine, abbreviated A, C, G, and T. A simple way to picture DNA and its units is to recall the snap beads most of us played with as children. Different colored snap beads could represent different nucleotides. Red for A, yellow for C, blue for G, and green for T. Nucleotides are strung together in a long chain to form DNA the way colored snap beads are strung together by young children. The four nucleotides function as letters that specify words, or codons, in the genetic code. The genetic code consists of three-letter words only. Four nucleotides in every possible three-letter combination results in sixty-four possible codons. Sixty-one of these codons specify another type of unit building block, an amino acid. Amino acids linked together form long molecules of amino acids called proteins. Proteins do work in the cell and are the reason that genes form distinguishable traits. The conversion of a sequence of nucleotides in DNA to a sequence of amino acids in a protein occurs through an intermediate—RNA. RNA is chemically similar to DNA.

---

9. "Genome Information by Organism," National Center for Biotechnology Information at the US National Library of Medicine, https://tinyurl.com/y6wwd798.

Both are nucleic acids. One difference is that RNA uses the unit uracil (U) instead of thymine (T). The process of synthesizing RNA using the sequence of nucleotides in DNA is called transcription—a word that indicates a form of copying that stays within the language of nucleic acids. The process of converting the information in a molecule of RNA to a protein is called translation to indicate a change in languages—from the language of nucleic acids to the language of proteins. One codon, ATG, functions to insert the amino acid methionine and as a signal to start translation, much like an upper-case letter at the beginning of a sentence. Three codons serve as signals to stop translation, like a period at the end of a sentence. All the rest of the sixty codons specify one of twenty amino acids (units). There is redundancy in this code. Some amino acids are specified by two codons and some by as many as six. Transcribed RNA molecules find large structures in cells called ribosomes. Ribosomes are protein-making factories. They read the codons in a messenger RNA and translate each codon into an amino acid in the new language of proteins. In translation (protein synthesis), ribosomes place amino acids into another linear molecule (a protein) in the order directed by the codon words of nucleic acid. This process, called the central dogma of biology, is illustrated in Figure 3.3.

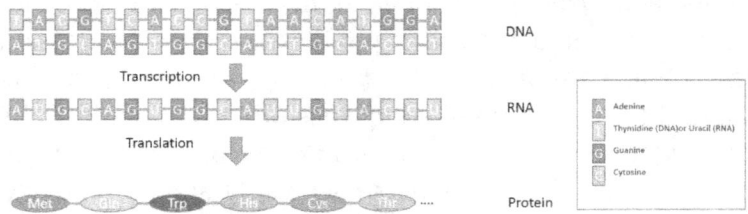

Figure 3.3. The central dogma of biology illustrates the relationship between DNA, RNA, and proteins.

The DNA in human cells is found in forty-six individual molecules called chromosomes. Stretches of As, Ts, Cs, and Gs within chromosomes make up genes. Human genomes contain approximately twenty-five thousand genes scattered along our forty-six chromosomes. We can understand genes within our genome if we think about the structure of books. The sentences that make up a book are a good analogy for a gene within a large molecule of DNA. A book contains many sentences. We look for start signals so we know where a sentence begins: a space that precedes an upper-case letter. Similarly, a gene contains the information to begin and end transcription and translation. Proteins in cells recognize start and stop signals so that genes are properly expressed. RNA polymerase reads the nucleotides in genes and synthesizes an RNA molecule that is complementary to the template DNA molecule (Figure 3.3). The RNA molecule attaches to ribosomes, which catalyze the process of translation, adding amino acids in a linear fashion according to the sequence of codons in the RNA to produce a protein. Proteins function as enzymes or molecular channels and gates, as signals within and outside cells, and for structure or movement.

The Human Genome Project revealed that human cells have about twenty-five thousand genes. Most of these genes can be processed in such a way (alternative splicing) that they can encode several related, but different proteins. Surprisingly, our twenty-five thousand genes make up only about 10 percent of the DNA in our cells. The rest of our DNA consists of sequences of nucleotides that serve as start and stop signals for transcription and translation, regulate the levels and timing of gene expression, or whose function we do not yet understand. Now that we have had a brief genetics lesson, we are ready to look at what genetics can tell us about human evolution.

Genetics and Evolution

Genetics says that the population of modern humans was never smaller than about ten thousand individuals and that these ten thousand individuals lived two hundred thousand to four hundred thousand years ago. Genetics also tells us about our closest living relatives, placing humans as evolutionary relatives of other primates. The evidence suggests that we shared a common ancestor with chimpanzees and bonobos about seven to eight million years ago and with gorillas between eight and nineteen million years ago.[10] Before exploring the evidence for these claims, I would like to clarify what it means to share a common ancestor to avoid the common misunderstanding that underlies the question my aunt posed at our family gathering, "You mean like humans came from monkeys?"

I am the daughter of Stan and Rhea. I am the granddaughter of Dave, Agnes, Austin, and Harriet. All six of these people are my direct ancestors. In my DNA, I carry segments of nucleotide sequence that came directly from each of them. I can continue back to my great-grandparents or great-great-grandparents and the same is true, although the amount of DNA I carry that can be directly attributed to each of them is less as I move back through the generations. I have many more relatives from whom I do not directly descend: aunts, uncles, and cousins, for example.

A few years ago, my husband and I decided to get our DNA tested through the company 23andMe. In addition to health information, 23andMe provides ancestry information. Potential genetic ancestors can use the 23andMe web-

---

10. Kevin E. Langergraber et al., "Generation Times in Wild Chimpanzees and Gorillas Suggest Earlier Divergence Times in Great Ape and Human Evolution," *Proceedings of the National Academy of Sciences* 109, no. 39 (September 25, 2012): 15,716, https://doi.org/10.1073/pnas.1211740109.

site to try to connect with 23andMe users that share segments of DNA and, thus, are likely genetic relatives. For months, I ignored the emails that came across my screen saying I had a new DNA relative discovered by comparing my DNA to someone else who was tested by 23andMe. One day, however, I got a notification that caught my attention. It was from someone with whom 0.82 percent of my DNA consisted of stretches of complete sequence identity. These stretches of complete sequence identity are most easily interpreted as segments inherited from a common ancestor. To provide some perspective, my first cousin, Jeremy, had his DNA tested by 23andMe, and 10.5 percent of our DNA consists of long stretches of complete sequence identity—segments we each inherited from our shared grandparents, Dave and Agnes. The 0.82 percent I shared with this potential relative was significant but not enough to catch my interest. What caught my attention was the contents of the third message. In this message, the sender indicated that her relatives immigrated to the United States from the Netherlands, and she listed the surnames of her relatives. One of the names she listed was Fikse. My relatives emigrated from the Netherlands, and Fikse was my maternal grandmother's maiden name. Now I was interested. We exchanged several additional messages, and I discovered that she has done quite a bit of work investigating her (our) family's ancestry. In her ancestry work, she traveled to the farm in the Netherlands her ancestors left to come to the United States several years ago and there was given a book of the Fikse family history. I was in that book! My four-times great-grandparents are her three-times great-grandparents (Figure 3.4).

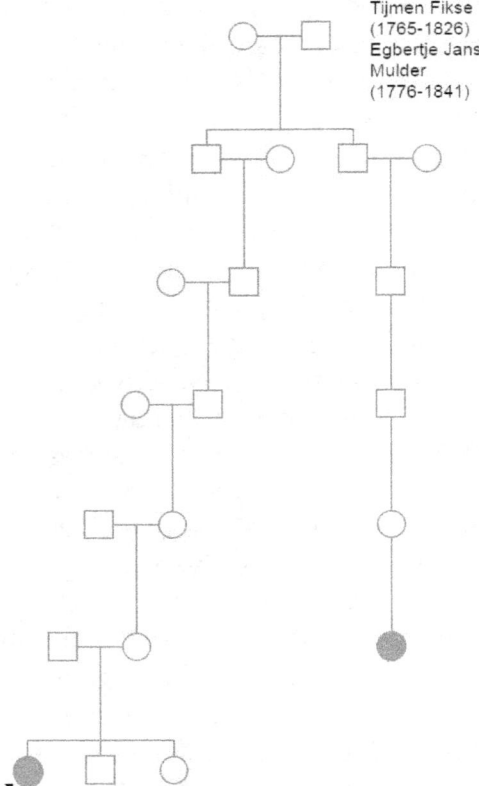

Figure 3.4. Fikse family pedigree. The grey circle with the arrowhead represents Sara (author). The other grey circle represents her 23andMe relative.

The common ancestors we share are Tijmen Fikse (1765–1826) and Egbertje Jans Mulder (1776–1841). I examined the 23andMe results more closely and found that this newly discovered fourth cousin once removed and I share sections of DNA on chromosomes 4, 5, 6, and 7. We each directly inherited these sections of DNA (and perhaps others we do not share) from Tijmen and Egbertje because we are each direct descendants of Tijmen and Egbertje.

Neither of us inherited these common sections of DNA from one another. Similarly, Jeremy and I directly inherited sections of DNA from Dave and Agnes. Again, neither of us inherited these common sections of DNA from one another. In both cases, we are *genetic relatives* but *not direct descendants*. The amount of sequence identity is different in the two cases (10.5 percent vs. 0.82 percent) because I have to move back through our shared ancestral tree further for a fourth cousin once removed (Figure 3.4) than I do for my first cousin, Jeremy (Figure 3.5).

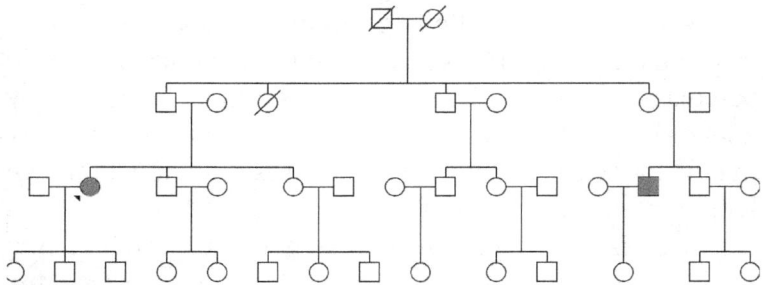

Figure 3.5. Author's paternal family pedigree. Grey circle with arrowhead represents Sara (the author). Grey square represents Jeremy (first cousin). The couple at the apex of the pedigree represent their shared grandparents, Dave and Agnes.

Similarly, other primates, like chimpanzees, bonobos, gorillas, and orangutans, are genetic relatives (not direct descendants) of modern humans. Of course, the ancestral tree and the most recent common ancestor goes back *much* further than 1765. How old is this ancestral tree? What kinds of evidence do scientists have for genetic relationships between modern humans and other primates? Are some primates more or less closely related? Now it is time to dig into the genetic evidence that supports these evolutionary relationships.

Evidence for Common Ancestry

The modern species with which we share the most genetic similarity are chimpanzees and bonobos.[11] Humans share more than 98 percent of their DNA with chimpanzees.[12] Chimpanzees and humans differ by about 1.2 percent while differences between humans averages 0.1 percent. It is important to note that these numbers reflect nucleotide matches over the entire genome. 23andMe percentages represent the proportion of the genome that has long stretches of identical DNA. Siblings generally show about 50 percent identity when measuring identity by descent. The 50 percent of nonidentity between siblings reported by 23andMe would still share about 99.9 percent similarity in nucleotide sequence with differences scattered along the large regions of nonidentity.

The DNA making up the human genome is divided into twenty-three pairs of chromosomes. Chimpanzee genomic DNA is divided into twenty-four pairs of chromosomes. One of the ways scientists observe chromosomes is by staining them when they are in their most highly condensed state (mitotic chromosomes) so they can see the alternating bands of light and dark and the constricted region called a centromere that is consistent between members of the same species. When we look at the array of condensed chromosomes from most humans, a karyotype, the only obvious difference between that person and another human is that

---

11. Kay Prüfer et al., "The Bonobo Genome Compared with the Chimpanzee and Human Genomes," *Nature* 486 (June 13, 2012): 527.
12. Chimpanzee Sequencing and Analysis Consortium, "Initial Sequence of the Chimpanzee Genome and Comparison with the Human Genome," *Nature* 437, no. 7055 (September 1, 2005): 69–87, https://doi.org/10.1038/nature04072.

females carry two X chromosomes and males carry one X and one Y chromosome.

When scientists compare human and chimpanzee chromosomes, twenty-two pairs of the chimpanzee chromosomes align well with twenty-two pairs of human chromosomes. The chromosome sizes, centromere position, and banding patterns are similar with one obvious difference. After lining up similar chromosomes, two pairs of chimpanzee chromosomes and one pair of human chromosomes remain. When scientists looked more closely, they saw that the two pairs of chimpanzee chromosomes, designated 2A and 2B, align with human chromosome pair 2. The banding patterns suggest that chromosomes 2A and 2B fused in a common ancestor to produce the single chromosome 2 we observe in human karyotypes. Scientists hypothesized that our ancestors used to have twenty-four pairs of chromosomes, but early in the evolutionary history of humans, chromosomes 2A and 2B fused to produce what we now carry as our chromosome 2. This fusion event occurred after we separated from the populations that gave rise to modern nonhuman primates, like chimpanzees, so they all still have twenty-four pairs of chromosomes. Are there ways to test this hypothesis?

The ends of linear chromosomes are called telomeres with repeating sequences of nucleotides that are indicative of closely related species. Vertebrate telomeres are repeating TTAGGG nucleotides.[13] If two chromosomes fused

13. J. Meyne, R. L. Ratliff, and R. K. Moyzis, "Conservation of the Human Telomere Sequence (TTAGGG)n among Vertebrates," *Proceedings of the National Academy of Sciences* 86, no. 18 (September 1989): 7049–53; R. K. Moyzis, J. M. Buckingham, L. S. Cram, M. Dani, L. L. Deaven, M. D. Jones, J. Meyne, R. L. Ratliff, and J. R. Wu, "A Highly Conserved Repetitive DNA Sequence, (TTAGGG)n, Present at the Telomeres of Human Chromosomes," *Proceedings of the National Academy of Science* 85 (1988): 6622–26.

end-to-end at some point in a species' evolutionary history, scientists predict that remnants of telomere sequences should be present at the point of fusion and those telomere sequences should be inverted—repeats of TTAGGG abutted by repeats of AATCCC (Figure 3.6). Here was a situation in which scientists could test evolutionary theory. Does human chromosome 2 carry this fusion remnant of end-to-end telomeres?

In 1991, scientists reported the results of this prediction put to the test. Scientists found the precise pathognomonic relic evolutionary theory predicted on the long arm of human chromosome 2 at band 13.[14] They also found evidence, at position 2q21, of an ancestral centromere suggesting that one of the centromeres in the fusion chromosome was inactivated—an event that ensured this new fusion chromosome was not broken during cell division.[15] These data provide strong evidence humans and chimpanzees share a common ancestor.

...TTAGGGTTAGGG-3'   5'-CCTAACCTAA...

...AATCCCAATCCC-5'   3'-GGATTGGGATT...

5'...TTAGGGTTAGGGCCCTAACCCTAA...3'

Figure 3.6. The expected sequence if two vertebrate chromosomes fused head to head. Upper panel represents unfused chromosome ends (telomeres). Bottom panel represents fused chromosomes.

---

14. J. W. IJdo, A. Bladini, D. C. Ward, S. T. Reeders, and R. A. Wells, "Origin of Human Chromosome 2: An Ancestral Telomere-Telomere Fusion," *Proceedings of the National Academy of Sciences* 88, no. 20 (October 15, 1991): 9051, https://doi.org/10.1073/pnas.88.20.9051.
15. IJdo et al., "Origin of Human Chromosome 2," 9051.

Another way geneticists use sequence analysis to understand evolutionary relationships is to ask what DNA sequences chimpanzees and other species share with humans and, conversely, which DNA sequences differ. These data provide insights into what makes us uniquely human and afford a glimpse into the evolutionary history of both species.

Orthologues are genes that are present in the genomes of different species. Orthologues share sequence and functional similarities. They are like words that are spelled differently in different populations but carry the same meaning (*color* and *colour*). Species that carry closely related orthologues share a more recent common ancestor. This similarity could be attributed to similar functional requirements, but pseudogenes cannot be interpreted this way. Pseudogenes are present in most genomes. They represent imperfect copies of functional genes. In the human genome, more than eight thousand processed pseudogenes have been identified.[16] Pseudogenes offer scientists another way to test evolutionary theory and to measure evolutionary relationships between species. Evolutionary theory predicts that species sharing a common ancestor will also share pseudogenes and that pseudogene sequences in more closely related species will be more similar than in distantly related species. This is precisely what scientists

---

16. ZhaoLei Zhang and Mark Gerstein, "Large-Scale Analysis of Pseudogenes in the Human Genome," *Current Opinion in Genetics & Development* 14, no. 4 (August 2004): 328–35, https://doi.org/10.1016/j.gde.2004.06.003; Zhengdong D. Zhang, Adam Frankish, Toby Hunt, Jennifer Harrow, and Mark Gerstein, "Identification and Analysis of Unitary Pseudogenes: Historic and Contemporary Gene Losses in Humans and Other Primates," *Genome Biology* 11, no. 3 (2010): R26, https://doi.org/10.1186/gb-2010-11-3-r26.

found when they examined the *NANOG* pseudogenes in humans and chimpanzees.

The *NANOG* orthologue is located on chromosome 12 in both humans and chimpanzees, as evolutionary theory predicts. Chimpanzees have nine *NANOG* pseudogenes. All pseudogenes are located on the same chromosomes in both species—two on the X chromosome, two on chromosome 6, and one each on chromosomes 2, 7, 9, 10, and 14.[17]

The number and locations of pseudogenes in humans compared to chimpanzees is consistent with the predictions evolutionary theory generates. Do the pseudogenes in both organisms carry similar mutations? This is a more rigorous test since there are many ways to render a gene nonfunctional, just as there are many ways to alter the recipe for baking a cake. If I added cornstarch instead of flour or left out the flour, the product I took out of the oven would not be a cake. Similarly, genes can become pseudogenes in many ways. An A (adenine) can replace a G (guanine), or nucleotides can be added or deleted completely. It is difficult to explain why two organisms would carry pseudogenes inactivated in precisely the same way outside of common ancestry. The *NANOG* pseudogene on the X chromosome carries twenty-one (of twenty-two) changes that are identical in the pseudogenes of humans and chimpanzees.[18] This similarity is akin to two people attempting to make the same cake but changing the recipe twenty-two times with twenty-one of those changes being the same. It is hard to explain this situation without invoking a scenario in which both people inherited a recipe containing the same

---

17. Daniel J. Fairbanks and Peter J. Maughan, "Evolution of the *NANOG* Pseudogene Family in the Human and Chimpanzee Genomes," *BMC Evolutionary Biology* 6 (February 9, 2006): 12, https://doi.org/10.1186/1471-2148-6-12.
18. Fairbanks and Maughan, "Evolution of the *NANOG* Pseudogene," 12.

twenty-one changes and then each made one, independent change of their own.

Humans are part of the evolutionary process. Humans are part of a creation that is on the way. These data also make it is difficult to argue that our genomes were designed as they are found today. Why would a God who promises in Romans 1:20 that "ever since the creation of the world [God's] eternal power and divine nature, invisible though they are, have been understood and seen through the things he has made," trick us? If all species were specially created, why include identical defects in primate pseudogenes? There are many ways to disrupt gene function. The simplest way to explain these data is common ancestry.

Are these the only data that support humans as part of the evolutionary story? Not at all. Genetic data that examines the sequences of olfactory (smell) receptors, the genetics of skin color, vitellogenin genes, and the discovery of Neanderthal and Denisovan DNA within human genomes all support the claim that humans are part of the evolutionary story.[19] Science observes that the story of humans is one of a species that is an intimate part of the rest of creation

---

19. Graham M. Hughes, Emma C. Teeling, and Desmond G Higgins, "Loss of Olfactory Receptor Function in Hominin Evolution," *PLoS ONE* 9, no. 1 (2014): https://doi.org/10.1371/journal.pone.0084714; R. A. Sturm, "Molecular Genetics of Human Pigmentation Diversity," *Human Molecular Genetics* 18 (2009); Roderick Nigel Finn, Jelena Kolarevic, Heidi Kongshaug, and Frank Nilsen, "Evolution and Differential Expression of a Vertebrate Vitellogenin Gene Cluster," *BMC Evolutionary Biology* 9 (January 5, 2009): 2, https://doi.org/10.1186/1471-2148-9-2; Benjamin Vernot and Joshua M. Akey, "Resurrecting Surviving Neandertal Lineages from Modern Human Genomes," *Science* 343, no. 6174 (February 28, 2014): 1017–21, https://doi.org/10.1126/science.1245938; David Reich et al., "Denisova Admixture and the First Modern Human Dispersals into Southeast Asia and Oceania," *American Journal of Human Genetics* 89, no. 4 (October 7, 2011): 516–28, https://doi.org/10.1016/j.ajhg.2011.09.005.

and, like other species, is on the way—part of a process of gradual evolutionary change.

Let's dig a little deeper into our evolutionary past. How long ago did the common ancestor of humans and our closest modern relative, chimpanzees, live? This question is similar to asking about the common ancestors I share with my 23andMe relative. How many generations do I need to go back to find our common ancestors? Because asking about humans and chimpanzees goes back much further than the ancestors I share with my fourth cousin once removed, scientists cannot use pedigrees or family trees like I did with my family members. They use mutation rates instead.[20] When scientists extrapolate back, comparing the sequence differences between chimpanzees and humans, they calculate that we shared a common ancestor with chimpanzees, our closest living relative, around six million years ago.[21]

There is a lot of time between six million years ago and the emergence of modern humans. Scientists are very interested in understanding what happened during this time. What genetic changes contributed to making us distinctly human? This is a difficult puzzle to solve. Both genetics and the study of fossils inform our understanding of the emergence of modern humans. The picture that is emerging is still murky and changes slightly with each new discovery. In fact, new discoveries in 2017 led to a significant

20. Yali Xue et al., "Human Y Chromosome Base-Substitution Mutation Rate Measured by Direct Sequencing in a Deep-Rooting Pedigree," *Current Biology* 19, no. 17 (September 15, 2009): 1453–57, https://doi.org/10.1016/j.cub.2009.07.032.
21. Yoko Kuroki et al., "Comparative Analysis of Chimpanzee and Human Y Chromosomes Unveils Complex Evolutionary Pathway," *Nature Genetics* 38, no. 2 (January 1, 2006): 158; Helen Skaletsky et al., "The Male-Specific Region of the Human Y Chromosome Is a Mosaic of Discrete Sequence Classes," *Nature* 423 (June 19, 2003): 825.

revision in our understanding of the timing of human origins and in what the human ancestral tree looks like after our ancestors diverged from chimpanzees.[22] This exciting new information is an example of how the scientific method works. Theories are continually tested and revised in light of new evidence.

Until recently, fossil evidence for human evolution told a story of a species that originated in east-central Africa (modern Ethiopia) 195,000 to 160,000 years ago, contradicting genetic evidence suggesting that modern humans diverged as a unique species (with a population that never fell below 10,000) around 430,000 years ago.[23] In 2004, scientists began new excavations in an area of the Jebel Irhoud massif in Morocco left untouched by mining and previous excavations. They found and identified fossils they called primitive *Homo sapiens* and used two different methods to date the fossils. Both methods pushed the age of the primitive *H. sapiens* much closer to that suggested by the genetic data.[24] The fossils are similar to modern *H. sapiens*, but the braincases are more elongated, more angled toward the back, and the forehead is more sloped

22. Bruce Bower, "The Story of Humans' Origins Got a Revision in 2017," Science News, December 13, 2017, https://tinyurl.com/ycy2jqwf.
23. Ian McDougall, Francis H. Brown, and John G. Fleagle, "Stratigraphic Placement and Age of Modern Humans from Kibish, Ethiopia," *Nature* 433, no. 7027 (February 2005): 733–36, https://doi.org/10.1038/nature03258; Feng-Chi Chen and Wen-Hsiung Li, "Genomic Divergences between Humans and Other Hominoids and the Effective Population Size of the Common Ancestor of Humans and Chimpanzees," *American Journal of Human Genetics* 68, no. 2 (February 2001): 444–56, https://doi.org/10.1086/318206; Matthias Meyer et al., "Nuclear DNA Sequences from the Middle Pleistocene Sima de Los Huesos Hominins," *Nature* 531, no. 7595 (March 2016): 504–7, https://doi.org/10.1038/nature17405.
24. Daniel Richter et al., "The Age of the Hominin Fossils from Jebel Irhoud, Morocco, and the Origins of the Middle Stone Age," *Nature* 546, no. 7657 (June 2017): 293–96, https://doi.org/10.1038/nature22335.

than that of modern humans. These anatomical traits are associated with important differences in brain anatomy and function.[25] The fossils are not Neanderthals either. The sizes and shapes of the facial bones are modern human–like, and the lower jaw is more like *H. sapiens* than it is like Neanderthals. These data push the date of the earliest *H. sapiens* fossils back to around three hundred thousand years old and begin to paint a picture both consistent with slow change and more consistent with the genetic data.

Supporting the Jebel Irhoud findings, a group of Israeli scientists recently discovered a portion of a modern human skull at Misliya Cave, Israel. They used three independent methods to date the skull at 177,000 to 194,000 years old.[26] Their discovery is the oldest modern human fossil outside of Africa to date and suggests that *Homo sapiens* migrated out of Africa at least 220,000 years ago. This date is consistent with the emergence of *H. sapiens* 300,000 years ago in Africa. Additional evidence of humans in Australia and Sumatra 73,000 and 63,000 years ago also support an earlier migration date out of Africa.[27] The revised dates these new fossils represent for the beginning of human evolution are more consistent with genetic data.[28]

What do all these data suggest about human origins? The

---

25. Michael D. Gregory et al., "Neanderthal-Derived Genetic Variation Shapes Modern Human Cranium and Brain," *Scientific Reports* 7, no. 1 (July 24, 2017): 6308, https://doi.org/10.1038/s41598-017-06587-0.
26. Israel Hershkovitz et al., "The Earliest Modern Humans Outside Africa," *Science* 359, no. 6374 (January 26, 2018): 456–59, https://doi.org/10.1126/science.aap8369.
27. Chris Clarkson et al., "Human Occupation of Northern Australia by 65,000 Years Ago," *Nature* 547 (July 19, 2017): 306; K. E. Westaway et al., "An Early Modern Human Presence in Sumatra 73,000–63,000 Years Ago," *Nature* 548 (2017): 322–25.
28. Lee R. Berger, John Hawks, Paul H. G. M. Dirks, Marina Elliott, and Eric M.

story of human evolutionary origins is branchy, messy, and incomplete. However, that you and I are part of the evolutionary story is considerably clearer. Our story, like the peppered moth, is full of imperfections (mutations), some of which were opportunities along the way. The features and behaviors we identify as those of modern humans are a mosaic of incremental changes over a very long time.

Christians who embrace the theory of evolution see evolution as the process God uses to create the wonderful biodiversity on earth. When Christians see themselves as part of the evolutionary story, they experience a deep connection with the creation, a connection we will explore in more detail in chapter 5. Scripture helps us understand our responsibility within that deep connection. Scripture tells us that each of us is made in the image of God as embodied, physical representatives of God on earth, tasked with the responsibility to govern and nurture God's good creation. We are an intimate part of creation, set apart from it by God's claim on our embodied, created identities as responsible image bearers. The role of humans as both a part of and set apart from can reorient us as relational beings.

Our relationships with the rest of creation are also reoriented in light of seeing ourselves as part of the evolutionary story. In evolutionary theory, we recognize that we are made of the same dust as all of creation. Biologists might call this dust DNA, the adenine, guanine, cytosine, and thymine we share with all other living creatures. Our call to ensure that God's good creation thrives comes from the creation to us, creatures who we are made of the very same dust. Our call also comes from God through Scripture

---

Roberts, "*Homo naledi* and Pleistocene Hominin Evolution in Subequatorial Africa," *eLife* 6 (May 9, 2017): https://doi.org/10.7554/eLife.24234.

tasking humanity with responsibility for the creation God loves.[29]

My aunt's question, "You mean like humans came from monkeys?" is a complicated one. One answer is, no, evolutionary theory does not suggest humans came from monkeys. Evolutionary theory suggests that humans and other primates share a common ancestor. At another level, the answer is, yes, humans, monkeys, starfish, oak trees, mushrooms, and bacteria are all intimately connected. We are all the products of the beautiful, God-ordained process of evolution, composed of the same dust. We all use DNA as our genetic blueprint, and this blueprint is deciphered using the same code. We are all cellular. We are all creatures. No, humans did not come from monkeys, but our connection with them is deep. As deep as our connection is to nonhuman creation, we have an even deeper connection to other humans. Our neighbors are also part of the evolutionary story. Together we are physical creatures, embodied image bearers, the result of a beautiful evolutionary process. Together, we are all on the way.

---

29. Jim Stump, "All Is Dust and DNA," BioLogos, February 14, 2018, https://tinyurl.com/y9a7c5hf.

4.

The Cross and Creation: Saint Francis, Evolution, and the Love of God

Jason Lief

> We want a God who will Lord it over us and be superior to us, and when we can't find such a God we invent one.
> —Ilia Delio, *The Unbearable Wholeness of Being*

For three weeks in May, I accompanied six students on an Italian pilgrimage. We followed in the footsteps of Saint Francis as he walked from Assisi to Rome to receive the pope's blessing to begin a new order. Our trip began with a three day stay in Assisi. Our guide, Eduardo, took us from place to place to help us understand the life and spirituality of Saint Francis. One of the more powerful experiences was sitting in the small church San Damiano where Francis encountered Jesus Christ as he gazed upon the crucifix. He heard Jesus speak to him, "Rebuild my church," which he took to mean rebuild the dilapidated building he was sitting in. So, he went home, took some of his father's stuff without asking, and sold it. He brought the money to the priest of the church, who refused to take it, not knowing where the money came from. When the priest insisted he couldn't take the money, Francis threw it out the window. Eventually, Francis realized Christ was asking him to bring renewal to the broader church, not a particular building, though he eventually did restore San Damiano for Clare and her followers to live in.

The story of San Damiano is important for understanding the spirituality of Saint Francis. Most people know about his poverty, his love for the poor, and his love for animals. He's often depicted in paintings and statues with animals all around him, a symbol of peace and tranquility. While this is true, there's more to Franciscan spirituality that offers a deeper approach to faith for all Christians. The spirituality of Saint Francis was never disconnected from his embodied life; God's word came to him in the suffering humanity of Jesus Christ. For Francis, there was no getting around the incarnation by meditating on the being of God; there was no going beyond the humanity of Christ to true divinity—the incarnation of the Son of God in Jesus Christ *is* the true divinity and character of God.

The Materialism of Saint Francis

Francis came from a wealthy family caught up in the trappings of status and honor. As a young man, he was on the path to a successful life following in his father's footsteps when, while fighting as a solider, he was captured and kept in prison—a traumatic experience that transformed his life. Before his imprisonment, Francis had nothing but disdain for the poor and the sick, symbolized by his dislike of lepers. Upon returning from capture, something began to change. While on the road one day, Francis encountered a leper. While everything inside him wanted him to run the other way, he embraced the leper and gave him a kiss. As he headed on his way, he turned back to look at the person, only to find he was gone, nowhere to be seen. On the road that day, in the form of the very thing he despised most, Jesus Christ appeared to Francis. From that day on, he resolved to remain open to encountering Jesus wherever he appeared.

Too often, Christians engage the issue of poverty by focusing on the wrong thing. The conversation usually becomes an argument about what we should or should not own, or whether we should own anything at all. Or, we focus on which political candidate or party we should support. Christians get stuck arguing about the spiritual goodness (or lack thereof) of capitalism, socialism, and every economic system in between. Not that we shouldn't be concerned about money and what we own, but too often it devolves into a legalistic competition to see who's more spiritual.

This is the problem with many of the service projects and mission trips churches undertake. They either see the poor as in need of saving or they romanticize the poor, not recognizing the complicated entanglements of economic, social, and political systems. The poverty practiced by Saint Francis was different. Yes, he renounced the ownership of property, and yes, he privileged the poor, the sick, and the marginalized in his preaching and way of life, but this had very little to do with staking a claim on contemporary forms of economics or politics. The Christian community can, at times, take a hyperspiritual approach to questions of possessions and the poor. It's easy to misinterpret Francis's way of life as a lack of concern for this world, a spiritualized longing for some heavenly existence. Often, monastic movements and practices are associated with detachment from this world through ascent. Through practices of prayer and meditation, we let go of this world and ascend to what really matters—God. It's easy to interpret Francis this way, as someone calling us to let go of the material world in order to live in a higher, more spiritual one.

This happens in contemporary Christianity when life is compartmentalized. On the one side is our material life, our embodied, cultural life, and on the other is our spiritual life, the life of faith and our hope in Jesus Christ. Within the Protestant world, this way of thinking is referred to as the two kingdoms approach to Christian life. While this takes many different forms, what usually develops in popular practice is a radical separation of material life from spirituality. Sure, we need to be moral in our dealings with people, and we certainly want people to see we are Christians by the way we live our lives, but faith is not about this world; it's about something else. In this context, poverty is transformed into a spiritual emphasis on how we need God. We spend time with the poor and the sick to remind us about what really matters—faith and spirituality.

This is not how Francis understood poverty. While praying in San Damiano, Saint Francis encountered God in the crucified Christ. Through this experience, he came to see the incarnation as an expression of God's love for all of the creation—God bending down in love for this world. For Francis, to know God is to know the incarnate Christ; it is to encounter him in his life, ministry, crucifixion, and resurrection. The incarnation, for Francis, is not a plan B; instead, it is an expression of God's love from eternity. It is the outworking of the divine community of the Trinity—Father, Son, and Holy Spirit. Thus, for Francis, there is no abstract God, no unknown God existing in some detached form of being. Franciscan scholar Ilia Delio, in her book *The Humility of God*, says that for Francis, God the Father is never a "lonely figure, detached from the Son. What Francis understood is that the Son, Jesus Christ is always in relationship with the Father. . . . In order to come to any knowledge or relationship with the Father, therefore, Francis realized he would have to come to know the Son—even better—to become like the Son, that is, to become an 'adopted' child of the Father."[1] For Francis, the Trinity reveals the nature of God as community, as existing in a relationship of love that is a "going out to the other for the sake of the other."[2] Thus, the incarnation represents the desire of the Trinity to be in relationship with finite creation. According to Delio, the downward self-emptying of God in the act of taking on human flesh is the revelation of divine love for the creation and for humanity. It is a downward movement, a vision of God's love that the Franciscan Saint Bonaventure described as the "gravity of the soul; it is what pulls us toward God."[3]

Historically, the church has referred to the sin of Adam and Eve in Genesis 3 as the fall, which impacts the way we think about salvation. Interestingly, nowhere in Genesis 3 is the word *fall* used; it's been read into the text. Instead of a fall, Adam and Eve commit a big overreach. Put simply, they take what doesn't belong to them. God tells them not to eat from the Tree of the Knowledge of Good and Evil, and yet they do just that, overstepping the boundary between creature and Creator. The idea of a fall is steeped in Greek metaphysics. Humans enjoyed a spiritual life with God until they disobeyed and fell back into an animalistic, material nature. In other words, humanity fell from the eternal presence of God into the material world of change. Notice what this view of the fall implies—the spiritual is higher and better than the material. The continued reference to sin as a fall fosters a dualism within Christian

---

1. Ilia Delio, *The Humility of God: A Franciscan Perspective* (Cincinnati, OH: St. Anthony Messenger, 2005), 21.
2. Delio, *Humility of God*, 23.
3. Delio, *Humility of God*, 23.

circles—the body/soul split. This leads to an overemphasis on ascent where the purpose of Christian faith is to escape this material world. At the same time, everything about an embodied life—change, suffering, death—is equated with sin, so that salvation is interpreted as freedom from embodied life. Here, one can see how evolutionary theory is thought to be incompatible with Christian faith. Evolution, after all, sees change and death as part of the creative process. It's not bad; it's merely the way the natural world works.

So how should the Christian community think about humanity, sin, and salvation? Interpreting sin as humans overstepping a boundary changes the way we think about sin. In Genesis 3, the serpent tells Adam and Eve that "they will become like God." In other words, the temptation for humanity was to become more than what they were created to be, meaning they were trying to become something they were not. Biblically speaking, it is the upward movement that causes humanity to disobey God. Sin is not material life; it is about trying to become more than our material life. To put it differently, sin is abstraction, what the Bible refers to as idolatry.

This directional shift changes how we think about what it means to be human, the nature of sin, and the meaning of incarnation. Instead escaping our embodied, material life, Christians are free to embrace this material, embodied life as "good." The finite limits of the human creature are not bad; it's what it means to be a creature. Maybe death is not just a curse; maybe death also has a good and very natural function, to provide the bookend to our life so we can be a subject—a person with a will and a history. This means that human beings, from the beginning, were created to be finite—to have limited time. It also means that being human is not some idealized perfection, but to live a finite, embodied life that includes change, love, suffering, and (gasp!) even death.

This affects the way we think about the incarnation and salvation. For Karl Barth, the Christian God is "no universal deity capable of being reached conceptually, but this concrete deity—real and recognizable in the descent grounded in that sequence and peculiar to the existence of Jesus Christ."[4] For Barth, the driving force of this descent is love—God's love for humanity that causes God to "bend downwards, to attach Himself to another and this other to Himself."[5] Franciscan spirituality offers a similar way of thinking about created life in relation to God. It is the gravitational movement of salvation that follows God's descent in the incarnation of Jesus Christ. Instead of humanity ascending in order to break free from creation, God empties God's self in incarnation. Delio describes it in this way: "Creation is not a mere external act of God, an object on the fringe of divine power. Rather, it is rooted in the self-diffusive goodness of God's inner life and emerges out of the innermost depths of Trinitarian life."[6] This means the material creation is not something to be overcome; it exists for the purpose of reflecting, and being brought into, the divine life of God as the creature toward whom God bends. This is the meaning of the incarnation, not primarily a response to human sin, but the climax of creation. It is the pinnacle of God's movement toward the creation. Like Barth, Franciscan spirituality interprets the incarnation as the revelation of God's love for creation. Delio writes, "For the Franciscan theologians, the life of Jesus provides a divine clue as to the structure and meaning not

---

4. Karl Barth, *The Humanity of God* (Richmond, VA: John Knox, 1960), 48.
5. Barth, *Humanity of God*, 49.
6. Ilia Delio, *The Unbearable Wholeness of Being: God, Evolution, and the Power of Love* (Maryknoll, NY: Orbis, 2013), 70.

only of humanity but of the entire universe. The thirteenth-century philosopher Duns Scotus said that incarnation was too great a mystery to simply remedy a defect. Rather, from all eternity, Christ was willed by God to come in the highest glory. . . . Christ is the first in God's intention to love and it is because of Christ that creation has its meaning."[7] Because of the revelation of God's love in the incarnation of Jesus Christ, Delio argues that "every living element of creation, from quarks and leptons to atoms and humans, express the Word of God."[8] She goes on to claim that incarnation occurred in the very beginning when God "uttered the eternal 'yes' to a finite lover. All creation is incarnational."[9]

This approach to Christian faith calls for a spirituality that invites us to fall downward, to follow the example of our God in Jesus Christ and bend low in humility and love. The mark of the Christian community is the love of God that pushes us to love our neighbor, which includes all of creation. This changes the way we think about the relationship between the spiritual and the material. Instead of seeing our embodied humanity as something to be overcome, we see how God comes in Jesus Christ to embrace our humanity. This also changes the way we think about sin. Instead of a fall into the material world, it is overstepping our boundary as creatures. Sin is the abstraction of our identity and the identity of our neighbor as we seek power and control over the world. This has significant ramifications for humanity, as creatures made in the image of God and as brothers and sisters in Jesus Christ. Of course, Saint Francis, Saint Bonaventure, and Ilia Delio are not saying anything new. To better understand the connections

---

7. Delio, *Humility of God*, 50.
8. Delio, *Humility of God*, 58.
9. Delio, *Humility of God*, 58.

between their insights and youth ministry and evolution, we first turn to the Paul's letter to the Colossians where he connects love to suffering in ways that are still challenging for Christian communities today.

Salvation and Suffering

Colossians opens with a discussion about strength, wisdom, and power. Paul prays that the Colossian people might be "filled with the knowledge of God's will in all spiritual wisdom and understanding" and that they may be "made strong with all the strength that comes from his glorious power" (1:9, 11). The letter ends with these simple words: "Remember my chains" (4:18). What begins with a triumphant declaration of the victory of Christ ends with Paul reminding them where it inevitably leads. For Paul, this is not a contradiction. He wants them to understand the message of the gospel, which is the message of salvation. But it's a view of salvation that does not focus on substitutionary atonement or appeasing the wrath of God; instead, it's a message about God's love for all of creation that's revealed in the suffering of Jesus Christ on the cross.

The opening chapter includes a hymn declaring Christ to be the "firstborn of all creation; for in him all things in heaven and on earth were created, things visible and invisible, whether thrones or dominions or rulers or powers—all things have been created through him and for him. He himself is before all things, and in him all things hold together" (Col 1:15–17). Paul connects creation with incarnation, saying that in Christ all things are being re-created and transformed. He writes, "For in him all the fullness of God was pleased to dwell, and through him God was pleased to reconcile to himself all things, whether on earth or in heaven, by making peace through the blood of his cross" (Col 1:19–20). The hymn suggests that the creation had its beginning in Jesus Christ, it holds together in Christ, and that it is moving toward a future identity only possible because of the death and resurrection of Jesus Christ. Creation is the work not of some far-removed divine power but of a God who so desires to be in relationship with the creation that this God became a human being.

According to this hymn, the incarnation is not a response to sin; it is ground of creation that holds it together, calling it into its promised future. Throughout the letter Paul emphasizes that in Jesus Christ we see the fullness of God. He tells them not to be taken captive to "philosophy and empty deceit" because in Jesus Christ "the whole fullness of deity dwells bodily, and you have come to fullness in him, who is the head of every ruler and authority" (Col 2:9–10). Here we find that Paul's message is directed against what in Ephesians he refers to as the "principalities and powers"—forces that foster abstraction and idolatry. Paul wants them to know that these powers are not real; they are a part of the creation that is in open rebellion, claiming a power and authority that does not belong to them. Ultimately, these powers are grounded in a false story about the world and what it means to be human.

In the world of Colossians, the Roman emperors were the best example of these powers, as they claimed a divine authority to bring peace and harmony through great military victories. They used their own form of media campaigns to convince the people that the political and social arrangements of the empire were divinely ordained and that the emperors were the mediators between heaven and earth. They did this by depicting images of the emperors as victorious in battle with the approval of the gods. Paul uses the imagery of the empire against itself by declaring that it is not the emperor who brings peace and order to the cosmos, it is Jesus Christ, the true Son of God who is, as the hymn says, the image of God. These other powers—including the emperor—have no authority. But Paul goes further, saying that these created powers, once estranged, are being set free through the death and resurrection of Christ as they are reconciled to God. Paul says that God erased the record against them, nailing it to the cross. He goes on to say: "He disarmed the rulers and authorities and made a public example of them, triumphing over them in it" (Col 2:15). In Christ, the Colossian people have "died to the elemental spirits," so Paul asks: Why do you act as if they are still real?

Paul rails against every power, every regulation, and every form of religious and cultural ideology that alienate us from embodied life. He criticizes regulations that forbid handling, tasting, and touching because they suggest the true meaning of the created world is found in some higher spiritual reality. They foster artificial divisions and oppressive social structures, which Paul address when he declares there is no longer "Greek and Jew, circumcised and uncircumcised, barbarian, Scythian, slave and free, but Christ is all in all" (Col 3:11). Every category, every label, every attempt to name, is undone by the cross. Sin is the human tendency to impose upon the creation some higher principle, some grand scheme, some big idea. The gospel shows that God's desire is for the creation to exist as embodied creatures. This is where God resides—embodied in Jesus Christ, dwelling with humanity and creation. And this is what Paul means by reconciliation—through the saving work of Jesus Christ we are at peace with God, our neighbor, and the created world.

The cross, in Colossians, is not a form of substitutionary atonement, or God punishing Jesus for human sin. Instead,

Paul interprets the cross as the revelation of God's love for humanity and for creation. Paul talks about putting on Christ, he tells them to "continue to live your lives in him" (Col 2:6). Paul talks about being buried with Christ in baptism and being raised with him through faith (Col 2:12). He then writes, "Above all, clothe yourselves with love, which binds everything together in perfect harmony. And let the peace of Christ rule in your hearts, to which indeed you were called in the one body" (Col 3:14–15).

Through all of this, Paul shows the Colossian people the deep connection between creation and incarnation. God takes on human flesh in Jesus Christ to reveal who God is and what it means to live as human beings in relationship with God. The life, death, and resurrection of Jesus shows God's love for human beings and all creation. But Paul is also clear that the creation is an expression of God's love. The incarnate Christ is the Word spoken in the beginning that brings forth creation, and this same incarnate Word is the means by which creation is now being reconciled to God. The death and resurrection of Jesus Christ is the revelation of divine love that seeks the flourishing of every part of the created world; it is the revelation of love that seeks justice, mercy, and freedom where there is violence and oppression. It is a love that insists on embodiment, embracing our finite existence, affirming our quirkiness. There is no ideal, no "perfect," no abstraction that we have to live into. The crucified Christ shows us how God embraces our finite existence and seeks to dwell with us in it.

So why does Colossians end with Paul telling them to remember his chains? For Paul, the mystery that he reveals to them is the mystery of the crucified Christ as the revelation of God's love. In other words, the cross shows us that it is suffering that brings reconciliation, it is suffering that sets us free, and it is suffering that makes possible a new way of life. This helps us make sense of what Paul is saying about his own suffering. He says, "I am now rejoicing in my sufferings for your sake, and in my flesh I am completing what is lacking in Christ's afflictions for the sake of his body, that is, the church" (Col 1:24). He is not saying that through his own suffering he's somehow saving the Colossian people—only the work of Christ saves us. Instead, he is talking about what it means to live as a new creation in the world; he is talking about what it means to live into Christ's death and his resurrection. For Paul, the way of God in Jesus Christ is the way of love. The way of love is always the way of suffering. Love is to be broken open for the sake of the other—to have all of our ideals, programs, and abstracts torn down. Love means becoming vulnerable, giving oneself freely, and receiving the other as a gift, with no transactions or conditions. For Paul, it is clear that love and suffering are always deeply connected. To love is to suffer for the other, and ultimately we suffer because we love.

Creation as an Expression of Love

The life and teaching of Saint Francis centers on the overwhelming love of God revealed in Jesus Christ. For Francis, it is the radical, self-emptying love of God that prompts Francis to abandon his family and cultural life for the life of a poor beggar and preacher. However, this is not just a spiritual program or social movement. What Francis encounters in the crucified Christ is not a different way to live within the cultural systems of his day; instead, he discovers a way to step outside of them. In the crucifix at San Damiano, Francis experiences what Paul describes in Colossians: the unmasking of the principalities and powers and the freedom to live into our humanity. This is what draws Francis to the poor and the marginalized—they exist outside of the social systems, unfettered and unnamed, pointing us back to our embodied humanity.

Theologian Leonardo Boff addresses this in his book on Saint Francis. He writes, "The Incarnation is, for Francis, a mystery of divine sympathy and empathy. . . . God feels passionately attracted to the interior of human nature."[10] It is this love and passion that moves God to action. First, in the act of creation to bring forth a world in which love and freedom cultivate the possibility of relationships. Second, in the act of incarnation that is the completion of the creative act but also the renewal and restoration of a humanity that has forgotten who they are and what it means to live as a human being. Boff describes how Francis "made clear a distinct way of being-in-the-world, not over things, but together with them, like brothers and sisters of the same family. . . . Because of this, the Franciscan world is full of magic, of reverence, of respect. It is not a dead and inanimate universe. . . . They are alive and have their own personality; they have blood ties with humanity; they live in the same Father's house as humanity. And because they are brothers and sisters, they cannot be violated, but rather must be respected."[11]

Bonaventure, like Francis, believed that God's presence could be seen all around in the created world. Delio describes this by saying, "Since the Word of God is expressed in the manifold variety of creation, Bonaventure views the world as sacramental; it is a symbolic world and

---

10. Leonardo Boff, *Francis of Assisi: A Model for Human Liberation* (Maryknoll, NY: Orbis, 2006), 24.
11. Boff, *Francis of Assisi*, 31.

one full of signs of God's presence."[12] To be human means not only recognizing the presence of God in the creation but to mediate the presence of God. To be made in the image of God is to live into this identity, as embodied persons that represents an outward movement of love toward the creation and toward God. It is to occupy the center, mediating the presence of creation to God and God to creation. Thus, the true nature of humanity is love, reflecting the nature of God as the one who brought forth creation in an act of self-emptying love.

Sin, for Francis and for Bonaventure, is to forget what it means to be human. It is to lose our place at the center, no longer loving but controlling, no longer mediating but dominating. Thus, sin is the distortion of what it means to be human in the world. Every form of sin flows from this distortion of identity, and it has real and disastrous consequences in the world. It is important, however, to recognize how Franciscan spirituality, specifically in Bonaventure, sees the relationship between the incarnation and sin. Bonaventure acknowledges that God comes to deal with sin through the incarnation. However, he does not follow Anselm's view that emphasizes satisfaction or payment to appease the wrath of God. Instead, Delio describes Bonaventure's perspective this way: "The Word became flesh to offer himself to all, to reveal truth and impart grace of healing. In the Incarnation, he writes, the eternal God has humbly bent down and lifted the lowliness of furniture into unit with his own person. . . . The broken relationship with God due to sin had to be repaired by the one who is truly God and truly human, and this is Jesus Christ. Thus, for Bonaventure, the Incarnation is a work of restoration. God became human in such a way that he could be known

---

12. Ilia Delio, *Simply Bonaventure: An Introduction to His Life, Thought, and Writings*, 2nd ed. (New York: New City Press, 2013), 61.

and loved, and in this knowing and loving God in Christ, we are restored in the image in which we are created."[13]

For Bonaventure, the primary reason for the incarnation is to make known the wisdom and goodness of God and to bring about the perfection of the universe. In other words, the primary reason for the incarnation was not as a response to sin but as a revelation of divine love in which God's desire for the creation is finally known. Delio writes, "The incarnation . . . is the perfect realization of what is potentially embedded in human nature, that is, union with the divine. In this way, Christ and the world are no accidentally related but intrinsically connected. . . . [T]he Incarnation completes creation."[14]

What Saint Francis and Bonaventure give us is a different way of thinking about what it means to be human in relation to the incarnation and in relation to the created world. Theologically, they provide a way for us to think about salvation and sin differently, affirming God's love for the created world and affirming our humanity as part of this world. What they do not provide is a way forward: How do we bring faith and science together in a positive, mutually affirming conversation?

Conclusion: The Relationship between Science and Youth Ministry

There are multiple approaches to the conversation between faith and science. In her book *Ask the Beasts*, Elizabeth Johnson describes them all the way from conflict to cooperation. She argues for a dialogue in which "science and

---

13. Delio, *Simply Bonaventure*, 89.
14. Ilia Delio, *Christ in Evolution* (Maryknoll, NY: Orbis, 2008), 190.

religion agree that they are distinct fields of endeavor, but rather than consider the other hostile or irrelevant, they approach each other with interested respect. While they cannot answer each other's proper questions, a sharing of insights from one field to another may enrich or even correct each other."[15] J. Wentzel Van Huyssteen says something similar in his book *Alone in the World? Human Uniqueness in Science and Theology*.[16] Van Huyssteen believes that the various disciplines of human knowledge may have different reasoning strategies, but every attempt to make sense of the world is always relational and contextual. For the Christian community this includes seeing the relationship between humans and the creation within the context of a relationship to God. Van Huyssteen puts it this way: "For me as a Christian theologian, this today means we have not understood our world, or ourselves, until we have understood them in relationship to God."[17] As with Barth and Bonaventure, framing our engagement of creation within the relationship between God and the world shapes our way of knowing. Reason never gives us objective facts with no context; we always receive the world in our own contextual and relational identity as human beings. The contextual nature of our knowledge influences the rational strategies we use as we explore the world. For example, a freshwater lake can be known aesthetically, focusing on questions of beauty fitting for an artistic approach; or, it can be explored from the perspective of biology or ecology. These different approaches use different reasoning strategies that ask different questions. And

---

15. Elizabeth A. Johnson, *Ask the Beasts: Darwin and the God of Love* (London: Bloomsbury, 2014), 10.
16. J. Wentzel Van Huyssteen, *Alone in the World? Human Uniqueness in Science and Theology* (Grand Rapids: Eerdmans, 2006).
17. Van Huyssteen, *Alone in the World?*, 8.

yet, they are different ways of knowing the one lake, which means that while they ask different types of questions, there are important points of connection.

For Van Huyssteen, these different ways of knowing provide the basis for interdisciplinary dialogue. He uses the term *transversal* to refer to where disciplines overlap. These overlapping spaces provide the opportunity for dialogue, either by asking questions of each other, supporting the results of research, or by challenging each other. The transversal space between theology and science includes the incarnation. The incarnation holds creation and redemption together, it affirms the existence of the material world and what we can learn from it, and it shows us God's desire to be for the creation. The incarnation affirms our existence as human beings, as embodied souls, and it affirms our cultural endeavors, including science. Van Huyssteen's call for the transversal engagement of science and faith provides a significant way forward for youth ministry to engage scientific questions, recognizing the limits of theology and biology but also seeing how they are deeply connected.

So what does this have to do with young people, and what in the world does this have to do with youth ministry? The answer is both nothing and everything. The expectation isn't that youth pastors become scientists—it's possible to do youth ministry well without giving a second thought to scientific questions. Yet, youth ministry cannot remain closed off from what science tells us about creation and what it means to be human. To be a good youth pastor means helping young people, and the churches we work with, to embrace the truth of incarnation. Research shows that young people (and adults for that matter) tend to believe in distorted versions of Christianity, which means that helping the Christian community to live into the truth of the incarnation is crucial for any pastoral ministry. The incarnation is what makes us Christian. When we realize that the incarnation is the basis of Christian faith—not whether the Bible is inerrant, or holding to a particular view of creation, or even holding to a particular view of how salvation works—we are free to take the creation seriously, take our humanity seriously, which means taking our embodied life seriously. Once we reclaim this starting point, testifying to the truth of the incarnation, we have entered the transversal space that opens the door to the sciences.

An open door is really the point. Inhabiting the transversal space and helping young people to inhabit that space goes a long way in demonstrating that Christian faith and science are not at odds. It establishes the dialogue approach advocated by Elizabeth Johnson, allowing the Christian community to ask biblical and theological questions of science and to ask scientific questions of the Bible and theology. The incarnation prevents the different forms of rationality that exist within science and theology from becoming absolutely distinct in a way that they are cut off from each other. Here, Bonhoeffer's assertion of the centrality of Christ for human existence means that the incarnation and creation are deeply connected. This means that scientific and theological questions are also deeply connected, even as they provide different ways of understanding the human condition.

So, what does this mean practically for youth ministry? It's not too difficult to see that the lives of young people in North America are increasingly directed away from embodied, material existence. We see this played out in social media, virtual reality, and even Spotify or iTunes, but it is embedded into the world of educational institutions, athletics, and yes, even the church. Lately, it seems like the Christian community is content to live in an abstract world of hyperspirituality that leaves the material world behind. We hold out the higher moral, doctrinal, and cultural principles we want young people to live up to and then reinforce those principles with religious language. This happens on both sides of the conservative/liberal divide. Progressives try to make the gospel relevant in a way that often blindly accepts the ideals of culture, while the conservative reaction is to hold tightly to doctrinal or ethical positions that they fail to see are much more cultural than biblical. Both sides lead with their own view of how the world should be and then use the Bible or theology to justify it.

This reconfirms the dualistic approach to Christian life where spirituality focuses on an abstract afterlife or abstract ethical principles that are unable to address the realities of human life. This is the dilemma facing youth ministry as it seeks to provide pastoral care to young people both in and outside the church. This is borne out in the research of people like Christian Smith, Kenda Dean, David Kinnaman, and others focusing on how young people experience the Christian faith. This dualism encourages young people to see their humanity either as something to be overcome or as a part of their identity that has nothing to do with true spirituality or the gospel. In the end, Christian faith and the embodied cultural life of young people never have to intersect—they simply coexist on two entirely different planes.

Francis and Bonaventure provide a theological approach that can help young people see that the purpose of Christian faith is not to overcome our humanity but to reconcile our embodied humanity with our love for God. By focusing on human identity as the image of the incarnate Word—the mediating presence of embodied souls as the meeting place between God and the creation—young people are given permission to explore how their bodies, their biology and psychology, shape their spirituality and their identity. When they are given permission and encouragement to do this, they will find that biology does not contradict the biblical revelation of God in Jesus Christ. We will discover that the evolutionary evidence is very compatible with God's love revealed in Jesus. An important first step is to help young people understand that salvation is not first and foremost God's punishment of sin or having to pay some sort of debt. While these metaphors for God's saving action in Jesus Christ are historically significant, and even have some biblical backing, they are not the primary biblical or theological metaphor for God's saving work. This is important because it is necessary to help young people understand that God is not saving us from our humanity in Jesus; God is revealing to us what it means to live as a human being.

Theologically, to interpret the incarnation as the culmination of creation, as that toward which the creation has been moving from the beginning, opens up an entirely new way of interpreting the scientific evidence for evolution. The progression toward consciousness, which is a way of saying the movement toward human beings as the integration of matter and spirit, opens up the possibility of embracing science as the story of an unfolding cosmos guided by relationality and love, seeking fulfillment in the union of the divine and the material. All of the biblical themes support such a story, including the story of creation, the story of covenant, and the gospel story of Jesus Christ. While this is not a basis for apologetics or dogmatic statements, it shows young people the possibilities of exploring the created world in the context of faith. Far from being mutually exclusive, they have always found ways to interact, support, and illuminate each other.

Recognizing Christ as the center of creation overcomes the dualistic tendencies that exist within Western Christianity. To be human, both biblically and theologically, is not to be a body and a soul; it is to be an embodied soul. This requires a view of spirituality, not as something added to or extra in some way; it's not a hierarchy of spirit over body. Instead, spirituality is embodied; spirituality is material. Seeing the incarnation as the climax of creation demonstrates that God's desire is to be present in and with the creation through humanity. Think of how this changes the way we think about embodied life. Think about how this can transform the way we think about the dualistic tendencies that dominate the digital lives of young people. Think about how this theological perspective opens up a much more creative and imaginative engagement of the sciences by the Christianity community. No longer does there have to be some kind of suspicion or disconnection between them, and no longer are young people forced to choose between one or the other for the sake of intellectual or religious integrity. Instead, they illuminate each other, with Scripture and theology speaking to the love of God for humanity and the world in Jesus Christ, and science helping us understand a much bigger picture of what it means to be a human being made in the image of God.

This is the gospel that Paul shared with the Colossian people. That just as God brought forth life out of the darkness, out of the chaotic waters "in the beginning," making a space for his people to have a place to live, laugh, and love, God is now at work in Jesus Christ bringing forth a new creation. In Jesus God shows us how the very creation itself is marked by the cross of Christ—an act of self-giving love that privileges grace over strength . . . life over death. Paul reminds the Colossian people that they have been taken out of their prior life—out from the violence and oppression of the old order. Brought into the mystery of new creation that restores and transforms, once again making space for human flourishing, for love, for freedom.

> For in him the whole fullness of deity dwells bodily, and you have come to fullness in him, who is the head of every ruler and authority. In him also you were circumcised with a spiritual circumcision, by putting off the body of the flesh in the circumcision of Christ; when you were buried with him in baptism, you were also raised with him through faith in the power of God, who raised him from the dead. (Col 2:9–12)

5.

Tending the Garden: What Evolution Says about Our Future

Sara Sybesma Tolsma

> One touch of nature makes the whole world kin.
> —William Shakespeare, *Troilus and Cressida*,
> Act 3, Scene 3

Early in 2017, the organizers of RAGBRAI, the (Des Moines) Register's Annual Great Bike Ride Across Iowa, announced the forty-fifth ride would begin in my hometown. Nearly ten thousand people participate in this annual seven-day ride across Iowa. Riders begin by dipping their rear bicycle tires in the Missouri River and end by dipping their front tires in the Mississippi River. It draws nationwide media coverage and riders from around the world.[1] The forty-fifth RAGBRAI route was to be the third shortest, third flattest in the event's fourth-five-year history: 411 miles with just over 13,000 feet of climb. (No, Iowa is not flat.) RAGBRAI had long been on my bucket list so when my husband and I, newly empty-nesters, heard that the ride was starting in our hometown and was one of the shortest and flattest, we decided that it was now or never. We formed a team with another couple, invested in new carbon-frame road bikes, CamelBaks, helmets, and bike

---

1. "RAGBRAI: The Register's Annual Great Bicycle Ride Across Iowa," https://ragbrai.com/.

shorts, and started to train. We spent hours upon hours on our bikes riding on Iowa blacktop roads, bike paths, around lakes, and around town: we got in eight hundred miles before we left Orange City at 6:00 a.m. on a cool, foggy Sunday morning in late July.

One of the things I love about riding, especially the long rides, is being outside. Traveling by bicycle means you journey at a pace at which you can pay close attention to the created world. I hear the birds singing in the groves. I see dragonflies dancing in the ditches and try to count the innumerable shades of green in a cornfield. I pay close attention to the wind speed and direction, notice any ominous clouds in the distance, how fast the temperature is climbing, and my nose takes note when we pass an occasional feedlot (it is Iowa after all). As a Christian biologist who accepts evolution as the mechanism by which God created, I feel a deep connection with the world around me whenever I am outside. I am a creature, called out as God's image bearer, loved by God, on the way with the whole of creation. I share a profound relationship with the birds, dragonflies, and plants. We decode our DNA in exactly the same way. We share orthologues and pseudogenes. We are all declared good by our Creator.

I am more of a tortoise than a hare bicycle rider, so my team members are usually a few miles ahead of me. I am also an introvert, so the solitude is welcome. It gives me time to reflect and pray. In her book *Help, Thanks, Wow*, Anne Lamott distills all prayers into three simple types.[2] The help prayers are prayers of desperation, asking God to step into the messes we make, and the thanks prayers articulate our appreciation for God's help. The wow prayers express praise and wonder. I use these simple prayers as I

---

2. Anne Lamott, *Help, Thanks, Wow: The Three Essential Prayers* (New York: Penguin, 2012).

ride. The wind is at my back. *Thanks.* I see a bee flitting from one head of Queen Anne's lace to another. *Wow!* A small group of monarch butterflies descend upon a cluster of milkweed in the ditch. *Wow!* I take the curve ahead to see that the hill keeps climbing. *Help!* Cresting a hill in the morning I see the mist in the valley reflecting the rising sun, and it takes my breath away with its beauty. *Wow! Thanks!* My connection to the created world is reason to worship.

Although I welcomed the solitary stretches of my rides, RAGBRAI is, at its heart, a community event. Traveling at a bicycle's pace affords opportunities to chat with neighbors who are also on the way (as long as the hill is not too steep). I met people from New York, California, Pennsylvania, and Denmark. I talked with first-time riders and people who have participated in nearly every ride so far. I met young riders and old, singles and families. The connection we shared was the ride, which made me think about our deeper connection as fellow human beings. *Wow!*

RAGBRAI reminded me that I find identity in my relationship with the creation, my neighbors, and most of all the Creator. Pedaling across Iowa made it impossible to think about these relationships as anything but physical. Every muscle and joint screamed embodiment. Evolutionary theory, too, reveals our deep, creaturely connections to each other and the nonhuman creation. It reminds us that we are not outside of creation but a part of it. It helps us connect the material and the spiritual. Our embodied relationships with each other, with God, and with the rest of creation ground us and remind us that God's covenantal promise in Genesis 9:15 "is between me and you and every living creature of all flesh." An evolutionary worldview compels us to reorient our relationships with God, creation, and each other.

Evolution and Creation Care

In 1967, Lynn White Jr. published a startling essay in the journal *Science*.[3] White laid the blame for the degradation of the natural world at the feet of Christianity. "Both our present science and our present technology are so tinctured with orthodox Christian arrogance toward nature that no solution for our ecologic crisis can be expected from them alone," he boldly proclaimed.[4] While White's arguments are imperfect, it is difficult to exonerate Christians from their role in the ecological crises we see in the world today. Understanding our place in the evolutionary story restores a posture of stewardship of creation. If we believe that God specially created humans and all the rest of creation is here for our exploitation, it is not surprising to see us behaving in such a way that takes advantage of the earth's resources. On the other hand, if we understand that humans are intimately connected to creation, we might be more inclined to tend and care for it rather than exploit it. What would it look like if Christians recognized their intimate relationship with creation and lived out these relationships?

We are addicted to fossil fuel (Figure 5.1[5]). We use it to heat our homes, fuel our vehicles, harvest our food, light our homes, and make the plastics that pervade our lives.[6] Fossil fuels, oil, coal, and natural gas were formed millen-

---

3. Lynn White Jr., "The Historical Roots of Our Ecologic Crisis," *Science* 155, no. 3767 (March 10, 1967): 1203–7, https://doi.org/10.1126/science.155.3767.1203.
4. White, "Historical Roots."
5. Warren Dym, "The American Revolution: Energy History since 1776," American Security Project, July 8, 2013, https://tinyurl.com/y7ok8hm9.
6. "Fossil Fuels Still Dominate U.S. Energy Consumption Despite Recent Market Share Decline," Today in Energy, US Energy Information Administration, July 1, 2016, https://tinyurl.com/yck7koea.

nia ago. To understand the source of fossil fuels and their effect on climate, we need to explore the carbon cycle.

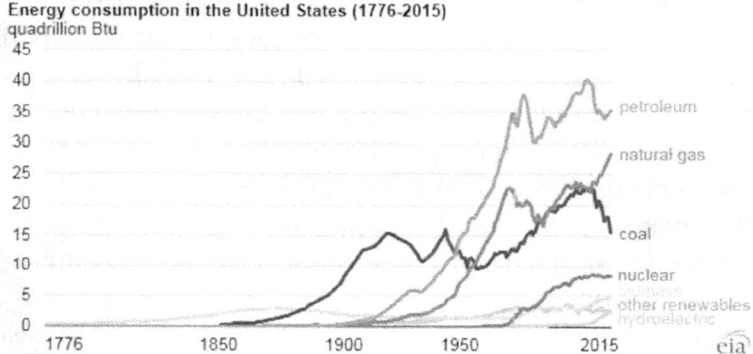

Figure 5.1. Energy consumption over time in the United States since its founding in 1776.

All living things contain carbon. The proteins in muscle cells, the energy molecule ATP, sugars, DNA and RNA, and the fats that provide the structure for cell membranes are just a few examples of carbon-containing molecules in living organisms. We find carbon in nonliving things too—rocks, oceans, and in the air around us attached to two oxygen atoms, as carbon dioxide (CO_2). Approximately 0.04 percent of our atmosphere is carbon dioxide. Carbon does not stay in one particular state. The carbon cycle describes the dynamic movement of carbon in the biosphere. Plants use carbon dioxide from the air, along with water and sunlight, to produce sugars when they photosynthesize. Animals use the carbon in plant sugars for energy, releasing carbon back into the atmosphere as carbon dioxide through cellular respiration. If dead plants and animals are buried in the earth for eons under great pressure, the carbon they contain becomes fossil fuel. The fossil fuels we use formed during the Carboniferous Period, around three hundred million years ago. In the absence of fossil fuel use, there is a balance between removing carbon from the atmosphere by photosynthesis and the release of carbon into the atmosphere through cellular respiration. However, when humans burn fossil fuels, we release excess carbon into the atmosphere and tip that balance. More buried carbon is released when we burn fossil fuels than plants can capture. If plants cannot capture the excess carbon, the carbon remains in the atmosphere. Deforestation exacerbates the unopposed release of carbon into the atmosphere when we burn fossil fuels since fewer plants capture less atmospheric carbon.

Carbon dioxide is a greenhouse gas. Greenhouse gasses function like a greenhouse—sunlight enters and warms the air, tables, and plants inside it. The glass prevents much of the heat from escaping so the temperature in the greenhouse is higher than the temperature outside. Sunlight entering earth's atmosphere is like sunlight entering a greenhouse. Some of the sun's energy hits the earth and reflects back into space. Plants absorb some of the sunlight and use it, with carbon dioxide and water, to produce sugars. Greenhouse gases trap much of sunlight's energy in the form of heat in earth's atmosphere. The heat trapped by greenhouse gases, like carbon dioxide, is necessary for life. Without greenhouse gases, the earth would be so cold it could not support life as we know it. However, too much of a good thing is not necessarily better. Scientists at the Mauna Loa Baseline Atmospheric Observatory in Hawaii announced in 2017 that carbon dioxide levels reached 405.1 parts per million in 2016[7] (Figure 5.2[8]). This translates to an increase of three parts per million, marking the

---

7. "Carbon Dioxide Levels Rose at Record Pace for 2nd Straight Year," National Oceanic and Atmospheric Administration, March 10, 2017, https://tinyurl.com/y9kca7d4.
8. Jessica Blunden and Derek S. Arndt, "State of the Climate in 2016," *Bulletin*

fifth consecutive year of carbon dioxide increases of two parts per million or more.[9] Forty other facilities, part of NOAA's Global Greenhouse Gas Reference Network, confirmed the Mauna Loa Observatory readings. Escalations in atmospheric carbon began with the Industrial Revolution, when humans started burning fossil fuel.

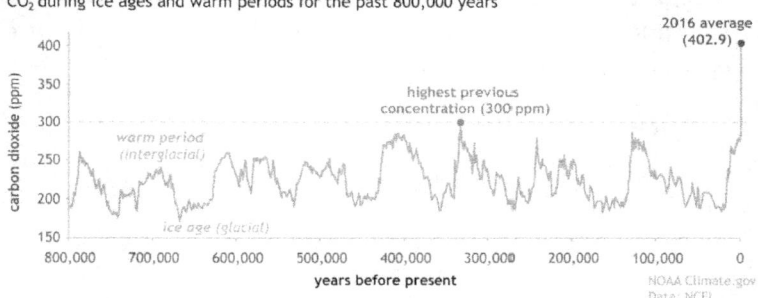

Figure 5.2. Atmospheric carbon dioxide levels over time show an unprecedented increase since the Industrial Revolution.

Excess greenhouse gases trigger changes in the earth's climate in a domino-like fashion. They trap more heat in the earth's atmosphere and average global temperature rises. The oceans capture some of the atmospheric heat leading to a rise in the average temperature of the earth's oceans. Warming oceans contribute to more extreme weather events. Water at a higher temperature takes up a larger volume, so ocean heating causes ocean levels to rise. Excess heat leads to melting glaciers, which also contribute to sea levels rising.[10] Dissolved carbon dioxide reacts with water

---

of the American Meteorological Society 98, no. 8 (August 2017): Si–S280, https://doi.org/10.1175/2017BAMSStateoftheClimate.1.
9. Scott Waldman, "Atmospheric Carbon Dioxide Hits Record Levels," *Scientific American*, March 14, 2017, https://tinyurl.com/y82ph82d.
10. Katie Weeman and Patrick Lynch, "New Study Finds Sea Level Rise Acceler-

to form carbonic acid, acidifying the oceans and causing coral reef destruction and damage to marine ecosystems.

Scientists have quantified the changes expected from increased atmospheric carbon dioxide. Most obviously, the average temperature of the earth is increasing (Figure 5.3[11]). The average surface temperature of earth rose 0.6 to 0.9 degrees Celsius (1.1 to 1.6 degrees Fahrenheit) between 1906 and 2005. Alarmingly, the rate of temperature increase has nearly doubled in the last fifty years.[12]

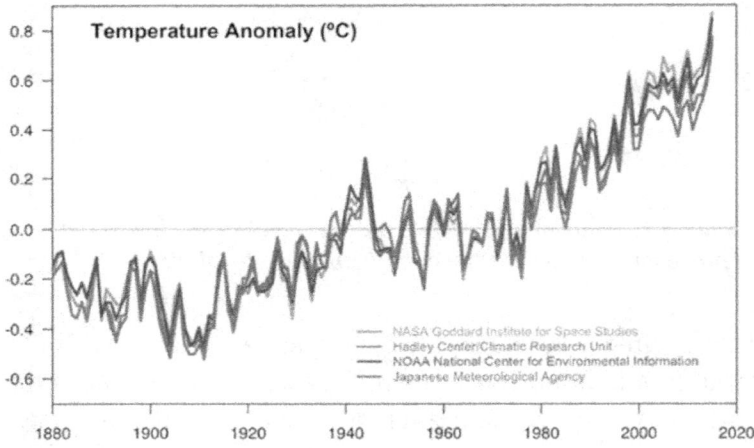

Figure 5.3. The average temperature, as measured by four independent agencies, is dramatically increasing.

A team of scientists from the University of Colorado at Boulder used satellite data from the NASA/German Aerospace Center Gravity Recovery and Climate Experiment (GRACE) to calculate how much melting glaciers are

ating," NASA Global Climate Change: Vital Signs of the Planet, February 13, 2018, https://tinyurl.com/ybnble6l.
11. "Scientific Consensus: Earth's Climate Is Warming," NASA Global Climate Change: Vital Signs of the Planet, https://tinyurl.com/y8ho3vm2.
12. Holli Riebeek, "Global Warming," NASA Earth Observatory, June 3, 2010, https://tinyurl.com/m93nq5n.

adding to ocean-level rise. Ice lost from earth's glaciers and ice caps between 2003 and 2010 was about 4.3 trillion tons (1,000 cubic miles), adding about 0.5 inches (12 millimeters) to global sea levels.[13]

Extreme weather events are not new. Floods, hurricanes, and blizzards have been a part of our weather as long as scientists have recorded it. The US Climate Extremes Index (CEI) has some of the best data about recent changes in the frequency of extreme weather events, and the data are sobering. In ten of the years between 2000 and 2018, the United States has experienced greater than average number of extreme weather events.[14] Another group of scientists measured frequencies and severities of droughts.[15] Their data are consistent with the CEI claim that the world is experiencing a significant increase in the frequency and severity of drought.

The oceans absorb about 25 percent of the carbon dioxide we release into the atmosphere from burning fossil fuels.[16] The National Oceanic and Atmospheric Administration (NOAA) reports that carbon dioxide has caused a pH decrease of approximately 0.1 in the oceans.[17] Because

13. Andrea Thompson, "Shock and Thaw—Alaskan Sea Ice Just Took a Steep, Unprecedented Dive," *Scientific American*, May 2, 2018, https://tinyurl.com/y9hssn4u; Thomas Jacob, John Wahr, W. Tad Pfeffer, and Sean Swenson, "Recent Contributions of Glaciers and Ice Caps to Sea Level Rise," *Nature* 482 (February 8, 2012): 514.
14. "U.S. Climate Extremes Index (CEI): Graph," National Centers for Environmental Information, https://tinyurl.com/y8jrhqxa.
15. Craig D. Allen et al., "A Global Overview of Drought and Heat-Induced Tree Mortality Reveals Emerging Climate Change Risks for Forests," *Forest Ecology and Management* 259, no. 4 (2010): 660–84, https://doi.org/10.1016/j.foreco.2009.09.001.
16. "Ocean Acidification: The Other Carbon Dioxide Problem," PMEL Carbon Program, https://tinyurl.com/kkg8bnt.
17. "Hawaii Carbon Dioxide Time-Series," PMEL Carbon Program, https://tinyurl.com/yc7hdwce.

the pH scale is a log scale, this corresponds to a 26 percent increase in the concentration of hydrogen ions over the past hundred years.[18]

There is broad scientific agreement that the earth's climate is changing and that human activity is the primary cause of climate change. In 2016, Cook and colleagues examined 11,944 recently published, peer-reviewed papers. An astonishing 97.1 percent of the abstracts that stated a position on human-caused climate change endorsed the consensus. "Despite the diversity of sampling techniques and approaches, a consistent picture of an overwhelming consensus among experts on anthropogenic climate change has emerged from these studies. . . . [H]igher scientific agreement is associated with higher levels of expertise in climate science," Cook and colleagues concluded.[19]

Our atmosphere and oceans are changing. Global climate is changing. The data are compelling scientists to conclude that human activities are the primary causes. Our failure to live in relationship with the creation has other harmful effects. Human activities are degrading fresh water.[20] Our misuse of land has caused the loss of organic

---

18. James C. Orr et al., "Anthropogenic Ocean Acidification over the Twenty-First Century and Its Impact on Calcifying Organisms," *Nature* 437, no. 7059 (September 2005): 681–86, https://doi.org/10.1038/nature04095.
19. John Cook et al., "Consensus on Consensus: A Synthesis of Consensus Estimates on Human-Caused Global Warming," *Environmental Research Letters* 11, no. 4 (2016): 5.
20. Mesfin M. Mekonnen and Arjen Y. Hoekstra, "Global Anthropogenic Phosphorus Loads to Freshwater and Associated Grey Water Footprints and Water Pollution Levels: A High-Resolution Global Study," *Water Resources Research* 54, no. 1 (November 8, 2017): 345–58, https://doi.org/10.1002/2017WR020448; Mesfin M. Mekonnen and Arjen Y. Hoekstra, "Global Gray Water Footprint and Water Pollution Levels Related to Anthropogenic Nitrogen Loads to Fresh Water," *Environmental Science &*

matter in our soils, a decline in soil fertility, alterations in soil compaction, erosion, changes in salinity, pH, the presence of persistent toxic chemicals, and susceptibility to flooding.[21] Air pollution is a global problem, and although acid rain caused by increased carbon dioxide shows improvement in the eastern United States, it is still a major problem worldwide.[22] Discarded plastics are accumulating at an alarming rate. It takes decades, at best, for plastics to decay. The plastic we discard remains with us well beyond our lifetimes.[23] Much of that plastic languishes in landfills, but scientists estimate that 15 to 40 percent of littered or discarded plastic enters the ocean each year, harming marine plants and animals.[24]

Human activity, such as building roads and cities, logging, and agriculture, leads to habitat loss and fragmentation, which risks extinctions. Like extreme weather, extinctions have been a reality throughout the history of life on our planet. Scientists believe that five times in the last six hundred million years the earth experienced a mass extinction. These previous mass extinctions were triggered by natural events such as volcanic eruptions and meteor impacts, not by the actions of a sentient species to whom God gave responsibility to care for the rest of creation. Yet, human-activity-driven climate change is leading to an increased risk for extinc-

---

Technology 49, no. 21 (November 3, 2015): 12860–68, https://doi.org/10.1021/acs.est.5b03191.
21. "Soil Degradation," New South Wales Office of Environment and Heritage, July 30, 2018, https://tinyurl.com/ybt5dqxn.
22. "Clean Air Markets—Monitoring Surface Water Chemistry," United State Environmental Protection Agency, August 6, 2015, https://tinyurl.com/y7tfl28p.
23. Marine Debris Program, https://marinedebris.noaa.gov/.
24. Angus Chen, "Here's How Much Plastic Enters the Ocean Each Year," *Science*, February 12, 2015, https://tinyurl.com/yckkxjy3.

tions.[25] Historic mass extinctions resulted in marked changes in life on earth. Given the evidence of extinction levels and risks today, scientists wonder what kinds of striking changes are in our future if humans do not make dramatic changes in favor of conservation.

World population data are perhaps the most sobering to consider. For most of human existence, population grew very slowly. The global human population did not reach one billion until 1804. In the past two hundred years, advances in technology, healthcare, and nutrition have enabled our population to balloon. As I write this, earth's human population has reached 7.6 billion, and it grows every day.[26] The impact of more than seven billion people on our planet means that we consume more food, fossil fuel, land, water, air, and minerals. We also produce more pollutants, greenhouse gasses, and other waste products, magnifying the problems we have already discussed.

Ecologists have known for a long time that environments have finite carrying capacities. Carrying capacity describes the number of living organisms a region can support without degrading the environment. Our planet has a carrying capacity. The carrying capacity of the earth is not rigid; technology can increase carrying capacity. For example, the advent of agriculture generated more food production from the same amount of land compared to the food humans could gather by foraging. More recent technological advances—pesticides, herbicides, hybrid crops, GMOs, and farm implements—have provided another boost to the

25. Mark C. Urban, "Accelerating Extinction Risk from Climate Change," *Science* 348, no. 6234 (May 1, 2015): 571–73, https://doi.org/10.1126/science.aaa4984; John J. Wiens, "Climate-Related Local Extinctions Are Already Widespread among Plant and Animal Species," *PLoS Biology* 14, no. 12 (December 8, 2016): https://doi.org/10.1371/journal.pbio.2001104.
26. "Current World Population," WorldOMeters, accessed May 14, 2018, https://tinyurl.com/3kw8txv.

earth's carrying capacity. However, carrying capacity is ultimately finite. Ecologists know that when a population exceeds the carrying capacity of its environment, environmental degradation is an inevitable outcome. And although there is no broad consensus on precisely what the carrying capacity of earth is, most scientists believe that seven billion people exceeds it.[27] Populations can surpass the carrying capacity of their habitat, but only for a short time, and during that time, they degrade their environment. Environmental degradation inevitably reduces the population when resources become scarce and disease more frequent. Environmental degradation leads to a long-term reduction in the carrying capacity of the habitat because it takes a long time to recover from habitat degradation.[28] If we translate this into what the future of humans on earth might look like, we would expect that the damage we do to the earth will result in a planet that can no longer support seven billion people or even six billion people.[29]

Evolutionary theory reminds us that creation is more than a backdrop for the human drama. Evolutionary theory calls us to reconnect theology and the created universe because "having evolved from this world, humans are a part of it, live interdependently with it, and by our actions affect it for good or ill." Evolution reminds us that we are created from dust, a part of the created world, and human life is deeply connected with the ecosystems and envi-

---

27. "One Planet, How Many People? A Review of Earth's Carrying Capacity," United Nations Environment Programme, June 2012, https://tinyurl.com/ya3vxq7u.

28. Wolfgang Lutz, "How Population Growth Relates to Climate Change," *Proceedings of the National Academy of Sciences* 114, no. 46 (November 14, 2017): 12,103, https://doi.org/10.1073/pnas.1717278114.

29. Jae Young Lee and Ho Kim, "Comprehensive Assessment of Climate Change Risks," *The Lancet Planetary Health* 1, no. 5 (August 2017): e166–67, https://doi.org/10.1016/S2542-5196(17)30084-0.

ronmental patterns of this earth. In the same way Scripture calls us to care for the world God created, evolution reminds us of our relationship with creation, which implies our responsibility to care for it.

Unfortunately, humans have not done a good job of caring for the created world. Humanity has been a poor steward of God's gift of creation. While not all of Lynn White Jr.'s arguments hold up to scrutiny, Christians clearly have not been at the forefront of creation care.[30] Christians are as much to blame for the activities that have damaged our environment as non-Christians. A 2015 Pew Research study revealed that white evangelical Protestants are least likely to believe climate change is real and (at least mostly) caused by human activity.[31] The same group of people are the most likely to reject evolutionary theory.[32] It is difficult to avoid seeing a link between the two. Many evangelicals do not trust the scientific evidence that supports evolutionary theory, in part because they are unwilling to consider different interpretations of the Genesis creation accounts. Fear of different biblical interpretations and lack of trust in science can motivate people of faith to warn their children about science and scientists. These Christians teach their children that science and faith are engaged in a bitter either/or conflict. Objections to evolutionary theory spill out into a general mistrust of science and scientists, including climate scientists who are ringing the alarm bell on climate change. Evangelical Christians notice the connection between evolutionary theory and climate change;

---

30. Wesley Granberg-Michaelson, *Ecology and Life: Accepting Our Environmental Responsibility* (Waco, TX: Word, 1988).
31. Cary Funk and Becka A. Alper, "Religion and Views on Climate and Energy Issues," *Pew Research Center* (blog), October 22, 2015, https://tinyurl.com/y8k3738q.
32. David Masci, "For Darwin Day, 6 Facts about the Evolution Debate," *Pew Research Center* (blog), February 10, 2017, https://tinyurl.com/y9kjcdu4.

both rely on similar kinds of data and similar arguments. It would be difficult, if not impossible, to accept one while rejecting the other. If these Christians cannot trust scientists on origins, how can they trust them on climate change? Therefore, an issue that Christians should have a natural affinity for—caring for God's creation—becomes an issue they must reject. Christians need to face the possibility that the failure to steward God's creation properly is collateral damage from refusing to accept the scientific evidence for evolutionary theory. Perhaps if Christians embraced evolutionary theory, taught young people to embrace it as well, and worked together to integrate an evolutionary worldview with faith, they would be better, more faithful stewards, and would reclaim a role as caretakers of God's creation.

In Matthew 22, Jesus teaches us that our greatest duty is to love God, and our second is to love our neighbors. Caring for creation is a way for us to love our neighbors—especially our most vulnerable neighbors. Christians from many denominations have issued calls for us to love our neighbors by caring for creation: the National Association of Evangelicals in 2011, a letter to Congress in 2013 from two hundred Christian scientists, and Pope Francis's encyclical in 2015.[33] "The Pope's unprecedented encyclical on climate change . . . makes a moral call for action based on the fundamental premises of the Christian faith—premises so fundamental that we can all, and must all,

---

33. Dorothy Boorse, *Loving the Least of These: Addressing a Changing Environment* (Washington, DC: National Association of Evangelicals, 2011), 29, https://tinyurl.com/y8oebadr; Katharine Hayhoe, "Why All Christians Should Heed Pope Francis' Call to 'Care for Our Common Home,'" BioLogos, June 19, 2015, https://tinyurl.com/y7ro7a8o; Pope Francis, *Laudato Si': On Care for Our Common Home* (Huntington, IN: Our Sunday Visitor, 2015).

agree," argues Katharine Hayhoe, director of the Climate Science Center at Texas Tech University.[34]

As the leader of the Roman Catholic Church, Pope Francis's encyclical invites all Christians, Protestant and Catholic, to consider the deep connections between environmental care and other social issues like poverty.[35] He challenges Christians who live among the global rich to consider the impact of using more than our share of the earth's resources upon both the environment and the poor. Climate change deepens the inequality that already exists in the world, disproportionately affecting those who are much more dependent upon the natural world for their survival. For example, mosquito-borne diseases such as malaria, dengue fever, chikungunya, and zika are especially sensitive to changes in climate.[36] Changes in climate alter the geographic range of the mosquitos, the length of their life cycle, and the frequency and opportunity for bites, which spread disease.[37] Breaching water reservoirs with rising sea water or extreme weather events can lead to an increase in water-borne pathogens like *Vibrio cholera*, the causative agent of cholera, in human fresh-water supplies.

34. Hayhoe, "Why All Christians."
35. Francis, *Laudato Si'*.
36. Hina Asad and David O. Carpenter, "Effects of Climate Change on the Spread of Zika Virus: A Public Health Threat," *Reviews on Environmental Health* 33, no. 1 (March 2018): 31–42, https://doi.org/10.1515/reveh-2017-0042; Nick Watts et al., "The *Lancet* Countdown on Health and Climate Change: From 25 Years of Inaction to a Global Transformation for Public Health," *The Lancet* 391, no. 10,120 (February 10, 2018): 581–630, https://doi.org/10.1016/S0140-6736(17)32464-9.
37. Jonathan A. Patz, Diarmid Campbell-Lendrum, Tracey Holloway, and Jonathan A. Foley, "Impact of Regional Climate Change on Human Health," *Nature* 438, no. 7066 (November 2005): 310–17, https://doi.org/10.1038/nature04188; Jonathan A. Patz and R. Sari Kovats, "Hotspots in Climate Change and Human Health," *British Medical Journal* 325, no. 7372 (November 9, 2002): 1094–98.

The poor have the least access to healthcare and for that reason are most likely to be adversely affected by these transmissible diseases.

A large percentage of the world's population is experiencing water and food insecurity. Freshwater resources are already depleted.[38] Cape Town, Mexico City, Jakarta, Melbourne, Fresno, and São Paulo are all planning for water crises they expect in the near future.[39] A number of scientific studies predict that an average global temperature increase of 1.4–5.8 °C, a range within what scientists predict is possible, will lead to a substantial reduction in fresh-water resources and an accompanying reduction in agricultural yield.[40] The poor are least likely to have the resources to mitigate the costs associated with decreasing water and food availability or to construct shelter that will withstand increasingly extreme weather events. They are the most likely to suffer the ill effects of increased pollution and toxic waste, and they are the least likely to have the resources to move away from areas that are especially vulnerable to the effects of climate change. We may already be witnessing how climate change disproportionately effects the poor in Hurricane Maria's destruction of Puerto Rico. Months after the hurricane devastated the island, thousands were still without power. Disease and injury stretched the healthcare resources well beyond what they could handle. Our relationships with the creation, our neighbors, and our

---

38. Jane Braxton Little, "Saving the Ogallala Aquifer," *Scientific American* 19 (2009): 32–39, https://doi.org/10.1038/scientificamericanearth0309-32.
39. Craig Welch, "Why Cape Town Is Running Out of Water, and Who's Next," *National Geographic*, March 5, 2018, https://tinyurl.com/ya7ccwfj.
40. Randal Jackson, "How Climate Is Changing," NASA Global Climate Change: Vital Signs of the Planet, https://climate.nasa.gov/effects; Anil Kumar Misra, "Climate Change and Challenges of Water and Food Security," *International Journal of Sustainable Built Environment* 3, no. 1 (June 2014): 153–65, https://doi.org/10.1016/j.ijsbe.2014.04.006.

Creator are intimately intertwined. To be faithful to one requires faithful relationships with all three.

Environmental stewardship is our Christian duty to the creation that God fashioned and loves. Stewardship is our duty as part of the covenant God made with us and "every living creature of all flesh."[41] It is also our responsibility to protect our most vulnerable sisters and brothers in Christ. When we help our young people embrace their part in the evolutionary story, they are more likely to see their stories as part of God's larger story. They are more likely to see that their story is intimately connected to the stories of the animals, plants, soil, water, and air of God's good creation. They are more likely to acknowledge that their actions affect the environment around them and the people they are called to love. When we acknowledge our deep connection to all of creation, we are more likely to modify how we live so that we are doing our part in responding to Pope Francis's reminder of our scriptural mandate to care for God's good creation.[42]

Evolution and Race, Racism, and Genetics

Christian faith through the eyes of evolutionary theory calls us not only to care for one another in light of climate change but also to bring reconciliation to human relationships broken because of our insistence on focusing on difference. Our species has a history of mistreating people because of differences in race, religion, ethnicity, culture, gender, socioeconomic status, sexual orientation, and educational level. Too often these differences have been used

---

41. NRSV Bible Translation Committee, *The New Revised Standard Version Bible: Pocket Edition* (New York: Oxford University Press, 2006), 15.
42. Francis, *Laudato Si'*.

to support segregation, hatred, and violence. Evolutionary theory reminds us of our similarities—we are all interconnected. At the same time, evolutionary theory tells us that difference is an important part of the created world as a source of beauty and diversity. An important example of this is how evolutionary theory reorients our understanding of race.

Archeological and genetic evidence clearly reveal that all modern humans originated in Africa. If all modern humans can trace their origins to Africa, where did the divisive concept of race come from? The word *race* was originally used to indicate a common genetic lineage or to describe a genetically distinct group of organisms, most often to refer to variations in animals and plants, much as we use the words *species* and *breeds* today. Although the word *race* was not originally used to divide humans into biological groups, attempts to classify people with different physical characteristics preceded the use of the word in these efforts.

Some point to the biblical story of Noah's cure of Ham in Genesis 9 and the genealogy of Noah's sons in Genesis 10 as the beginning of the concept of race. While the curse was one of slavery, the text does not include a physical description of Ham or his descendants, making the claim that this curse was race-based difficult to defend. Bernard Lewis, in his book *Race and Slavery in the Middle East*, notes that Arab slave traders in the Middle East were the group that first interpreted Genesis 9 and 10 to include differences in human traits, specifically skin color.[43]

Hippocrates and Herodotus introduced the idea that skin color was associated with climate. Aristotle and his followers formalized the idea as the climatic theory, which

---

43. Bernard Lewis, *Race and Slavery in the Middle East: An Historical Enquiry* (New York: Oxford University Press, 1992), 44, 123.

proposed that the physical and mental characteristics of people were determined by climate and that these characteristics were transmitted from generation to generation.[44] They believed that cold climates produced light skin tones while excessive heat scorched the skin resulting in dark skin tones. Aristotle, not surprisingly, believed that the climate of Greece was ideal, and since climate determined both mental and physical characteristics, he concluded that Greeks, in their perfect climate, embodied superior physical, mental, emotional, and social characteristics. He used this to justify his assertion that Greeks should govern, even enslave, other people groups—groups whose climate adaptations left them with inferior characteristics. The Spanish and Portuguese, engaging in African and Native American slave trade in the fourteenth century, justified their actions with Aristotle's argument. They perpetuated the notion that some people were born to be slaves, and they extended this phrase to include whole populations of humans, connecting slavery to race.[45]

In *On the Origin of Species*, Darwin uses the word *race* to describe variations within the species *Homo sapiens*.[46] However, the most common use of the word in Darwin's writing was to describe variation within nonhuman species, which he elaborates on in his book *The Descent of Man and Selection in Relation to Sex*.[47] While Darwin used the word to describe variations and, for that reason, is often accused

---

44. Nina G. Jablonski, *Living Color: The Biological and Social Meaning of Skin Color* (Berkeley: University of California Press, 2012).
45. Dave Unander, *Shattering the Myth of Race: Genetic Realities and Biblical Truths* (Valley Forge, PA: Judson, 2000).
46. Charles Darwin, *Origin of Species by Means of Natural Selection, Or the Preservation of Favored Races in the Struggle for Life* (New York: P. F. Collier & Son, 1902), 34–35.
47. Charles Darwin, *The Descent of Man, and Selection in Relation to Sex* (New York: D. Appleton, 1882).

of promoting racism, he was an outspoken opponent of slavery. Furthermore, Darwin opposed categorizing people into biological groups or species because groups of humans "graduate into each other, and . . . it is hardly possible to discover clear distinctive character between them."[48] Darwin rejected Aristotle's climatic theory. Instead, he preferred sexual selection as an explanation for variations in human skin color. In *The Descent of Man and Selection in Relation to Sex*, he wrote:

> If however, we look to the races of man, as distributed over the world, we must infer that their characteristic differences cannot be accounted for by the direct action of different conditions of life, even after exposure to them for an enormous period of time. . . . It can be further shewn that the differences between the races of man, as in colour, hairiness, form of features, &c., are of the nature which it might have been expected would have been acted on by sexual selection.[49]

Carl Linnaeus, a Swedish botanist often called the Father of Taxonomy, developed a system of classification of living things most of us became familiar with in our high-school biology classes. He published his classification system, the Linnaean system, in the *Systema Naturae*.[50] The Linnaean system places all living organisms into the increasingly narrow categories of kingdom, phylum, class, order, family, genus, and species. In the Linnaean system, humans are in the kingdom Animalia, the phylum Chordata, the subphylum Vertebrata, the class Mammalia, the order Primates, the family Hominidae, the genus *Homo*, and the species *sapiens*. In the Linnaean system, all humans are classified as a single genus and a single

---

48. Darwin, *Descent of Man*, 226.
49. Darwin, *Descent of Man*, 246, 250.
50. *Linnaeus—1758 Systema Naturae*, 1758, https://tinyurl.com/y9zj9xc8.

species. He further classified humans into four varieties: americanus, europaeus, asiaticus, and afer. For the four varieties, he used not physical characteristics but behavioral ones (tenacity, liveliness, haughtiness, and cunning, for example).[51]

Blumenbach, a German scientist, also proposed dividing humankind into categories in the first of three editions of his thesis. In his third edition, he proposed five generic varieties: Caucasians, Mongolians, Ethiopians, Americans, and Malays.[52] He attributed the variety he observed to differences in climate while claiming that variations in opportunities were the underlying cause of the differences scientists observed between people of different skin colors.

W. E. B. Du Bois, a sociologist, picked up some of Blumenbach's arguments when he contended that the health disparities documented between whites and blacks were due to economic and social inequity rather than biology. Du Bois went farther than Blumenbach, arguing that the concept of race was not a scientific classification.[53] Blumenbach's and Du Bois's arguments were ignored in most scientific, social, and political arenas. Instead, the science of race was often cited to defend immoral actions against people who were different. Scientists continued to believe that they would be able to find a way to measure some physical trait or set of traits and that they would be able to use these traits to place individual humans into definitive racial categories. They measured, probed, and categorized relative proportions of body parts, skin color, eye color,

51. Leslie Clarence Dunn and Theodosius Grigorievich Dobzhansky, *Heredity, Race, and Society* (New York: New American Library, 1952).
52. Daniel J. Fairbanks, *Everyone Is African: How Science Explodes the Myth of Race* (Amherst, NY: Prometheus, 2015).
53. Dominic J. Capeci Jr. and Jack C. Knight, "Reckoning with Violence: W. E. B. Du Bois and the 1906 Atlanta Race Riot," *The Journal of Southern History* 62, no. 4 (November 1996): 727–66, https://doi.org/10.2307/2211139.

hair texture, blood type, and head shape. The problem with all of these studies was that no single trait or set of traits reliably placed individuals in any racial category. Groups of people did, based on geography, show a higher probability of certain traits, but probability could not reliably place individuals in a racial category. There were always individuals that failed to fit the expected patterns. Scientists could reliably find more people with blood type B in northern China than in Italy, however people of all four blood types (O, A, B, and AB) were found in both populations. Having a particular blood type was not a marker of race. Scientists could reliably find more brown-eyed people in Mexico than in Sweden, but brown-eyed people were part of both populations. Eye color was not a marker of race. Neither was skin color or head shape definitively indicative of race since variations of skin color and head shape were present in all populations.[54] Du Bois and others were speaking into an environment that was embracing eugenics, and most researchers ignored their voices.

Where do the biological characteristics we most often associate with race come from, and how do these characteristics relate to humans as part of the evolutionary story? Let's look at skin color as our example. The observation that people with darker skin tend to live closer to the equator and people with lighter skin tend to live closer to the poles led scientists to hypothesize that skin color evolved to protect people from harmful solar radiation. This hypothesis prevailed among scientists for decades, and experiments that uncovered the function of melanin supported it. Melanin is a pigment produced by specialized cells in the skin called melanocytes. Melanocytes can produce two kinds of melanin in membrane-bound structures

---

54. Dunn and Dobzhansky, *Heredity, Race, and Society*.

called melanosomes.[55] Melanocytes transfer melanosomes to surrounding keratinocytes, the most abundant cell type of the most superficial layer of skin. Keratinocytes arrange the pigment-containing melanosomes like an umbrella over their nuclei. The melanin can then absorb ultraviolet (UV) light from the sun and protect the DNA in the keratinocytes from UV-induced DNA mutation.[56] Humans have very little variation in the number of melanocytes that are present in the epidermis. Skin color difference is primarily due to the amount and the color of the melanin produced.

The closest modern ancestors of humans, chimpanzees and bonobos, have light skin covered with dark hair. Scientists believe that as humans evolved, they lost the hair covering most of their bodies. Hair prevents sweat evaporation from effectively cooling the body, so scientists hypothesized that thermoregulation was the primary environmental influence promoting hair loss. Scientists who study the skeletons of the ancient relatives of humans believe that, before three million years ago, hairy hominids lived like modern primates do today: on the open savanna in Africa spending much of their days foraging for food. They searched in a range of only about three or four miles before retreating to the safety and shade of trees to rest. By around 1.5 million years ago, skeletons indicate that ancient humans, such as *Homo ergaster*, were bipedal organisms

---

55. John D'Orazio, Stuart Jarrett, Alexandra Amaro-Ortiz, and Timothy Scott, "UV Radiation and the Skin," *International Journal of Molecular Sciences* 14, no. 6 (June 2013): 12,222–48, https://doi.org/10.3390/ijms140612222; A. J. Thody, E. M. Higgins, K. Wakamatsu, S. Ito, S. A. Burchill, and J. M. Marks, "Pheomelanin as Well as Eumelanin Is Present in Human Epidermis," *The Journal of Investigative Dermatology* 97, no. 2 (August 1991): 340–44.

56. M. Brenner and V. J. Hearing, "The Protective Role of Melanin against UV Damage in Human Skin," *Photochemistry and Photobiology* 84, no. 3 (2008): 539–49.

with long legs and front-facing faces, indicating that they could walk long distances to forage and gather but also to hunt. Extensive body hair made it difficult for these active hominids to stay cool and selective pressure led to the loss of body hair as well as an increase in the number of sweat glands in the epidermis.[57] Without body hair, the exposed keratinocytes were vulnerable to mutation by UV light from the sun.

Chimpanzees, and presumably our ancient ancestors, have melanocytes producing melanin on the parts of their bodies that lack hair: their face and palms. Scientists propose that, in order to provide protection from the sun in the absence of hair, the melanocytes that were already present began to produce more and darker melanin in some hominids. Dark, hairless skin was an advantageous adaptation for the humans in equatorial Africa. However, as humans began to migrate out of Africa, dark skin was no longer as critical to protect humans from UV radiation because the intensity of UV radiation decreases as one moves farther away from the equator. In addition, dark skin plus decreased UV radiation became disadvantageous relating to the production of vitamin D. Vitamin D is made in the skin upon exposure to UVB rays from sunlight.[58] Vitamin D deficiency leads to rickets, a disease characterized by softened and weakened bones. The symptoms occur because vitamin D promotes the absorption of the calcium and phosphorus we consume in our diets. A deficiency in vitamin D leads to the inability to maintain calcium and phosphorus levels that are necessary for bone health. Thus, dark skin in a climate without abundant sunlight makes

---

57. Peter J. Brown and Svea Closser, *Understanding and Applying Medical Anthropology* (London: Routledge, 2016).
58. Rathish Nair and Arun Maseeh, "Vitamin D: The 'Sunshine' Vitamin," *Journal of Pharmacology and Pharmacotherapeutics* 3, no. 2 (2012): 118–26.

vitamin D deficiency and its associated health problems more likely. A new environment, one with less UV exposure, provided a new selective pressure. The pressure led to a selective advantage for individuals with decreased melanin production. Thus, lighter pigmentation became the more common trait, an adaptation we observe in humans living in geographical areas far from the equator.

This explanation for the diversity we see in skin color was widely accepted for some time, but persistent questions kept scientists studying the evolution of skin color. The most dogged question related to how this explanation fit with evolutionary theory. Scientists were increasingly skeptical that protection from mutation by UV radiation could exert evolutionary pressure because skin cancer that arises from mutations caused by UV radiation does not typically present until well after reproductive age. If humans passed on their genes to the next generation long before succumbing to skin cancer, there would be no selective pressure for skin color based on UV light exposure. Scientists looked for another answer.

In 1978, scientists proposed a new explanation for the gradient in skin coloration we see when we move toward or away from the equator, but it took more than twenty years to fully understand that skin-color adaptation was primarily to protect folate from degradation by UV light rather than to protect DNA from UV-induced mutation.[59] Folate (vitamin B-9) is involved in DNA biosynthesis and repair, DNA methylation (critical for gene regulation), and amino acid

---

59. R. F. Branda and J. W. Eaton, "Skin Color and Nutrient Photolysis: An Evolutionary Hypothesis," *Science* 201, no. 4356 (August 18, 1978): 625–26; David C. Borradale and Michael G. Kimlin, "Folate Degradation Due to Ultraviolet Radiation: Possible Implications for Human Health and Nutrition," *Nutrition Reviews* 70, no. 7 (July 2012): 414–22, https://doi.org/10.1111/j.1753-4887.2012.00485.x; Jablonski, *Living Color*, 9–92.

metabolism. Dark green leafy vegetables, beans, peas, nuts, oranges, lemons, bananas, melons, and strawberries are rich in folate. Many of the foods we eat are supplemented with folate, including cereals and pastas. Folate is especially important for pregnant women because it reduces the risk of neural-tube defects in a developing fetus. For this reason, doctors urge pregnant women and even women who plan to become pregnant to take folate supplements.[60] Folate circulates in the bloodstream where it is susceptible to degradation when it is exposed to the UV radiation that penetrates skin and blood vessels. Folate deficiency, as opposed to DNA damage leading to skin cancer, can exert evolutionary pressure because it causes decreased fertility in adults and severe spinal cord and brain defects in fetuses. Scientists put the need for vitamin D, generated by UV light, and folate, destroyed by excess UV light, together in a new hypothesis. Individuals with dark skin in a climate far from the equator are more likely to experience vitamin D deficiencies. Vitamin D deficiency can make it less likely that an individual will pass their genes on to the next generation. In climates with ample sunlight, dark skin is advantageous to protect folate from UV-induced degradation. Plentiful sunlight allows sufficient vitamin D production even with a high degree of melaninization. In climates with limited sunlight, however, light skin is more advantageous so that the skin produces enough vitamin D. Folate is not at risk of UV-induced degradation because of the limited sunlight exposure in these climates.[61]

60. Theresa O. Scholl and William G. Johnson, "Folic Acid: Influence on the Outcome of Pregnancy," *The American Journal of Clinical Nutrition* 71, no. 5 (2000): 1295S–303S, https://doi.org/10.1093/ajcn/71.5.1295s.
61. Nina G. Jablonski and George Chaplin, "The Evolution of Human Skin Coloration," *Journal of Human Evolution* 39, no. 1 (July 2000): 57–106, https://doi.org/10.1006/jhev.2000.0403.

Scientists tested the folate and vitamin D hypothesis. This hypothesis predicts that distance from the equator should not be the only geographical determinant of skin color. At high altitudes, the atmosphere is thinner than low altitudes, and UV radiation penetrates a thin atmosphere more efficiently. Persistent cloud cover reduces penetrating UV light regardless of the geographical relationship to the equator. The new hypothesis, therefore, predicts that populations living at high altitudes, even if they are far from the equator, should have darker skin to protect folic acid from the penetrating UV light, and populations in areas with persistent cloud cover should have lighter skin even if they are located near the equator. To test their prediction, scientists precisely mapped the radiation intensity over the entire globe. The most striking pattern they saw was the gradient of UV radiation from the equator to the poles, as expected. They also observed that some locations near the equator, such as the humid Congo basin, had persistent cloud cover, reducing radiation exposure. Other locations that are farther from the equator but are at high elevations, such as Tibet, measured high radiation exposure. Scientists measured skin color of people throughout the world and superimposed the two maps. The predictions aligned nearly perfectly. People living in areas of high UV radiation had darker skin even if they were far from the equator. People living close to the equator but in areas with low UV radiation had lighter skin. Scientists found one interesting exception to their predictions in populations of indigenous Alaskans who live far from the equator, at low elevation, and experience very low levels of UV radiation. Indigenous Alaskans have unexpectedly dark skin. Scientists were quick to note that the diets of indigenous Alaskans, which included oily fish and marine mammals, were high in vitamin D, eliminating the need for vitamin

D produced by the skin in response to UV light. To support this explanation, physicians see that recent changes in the diets of native Alaskans has been accompanied by increased incidence in rickets, supporting the explanation the scientists proposed.[62] Scientists have also used genetics to confirm the vitamin D and folate hypothesis.[63]

Data from the Human Genome Project have corroborated previous scientific investigations and concluded that classification by race is an oversimplified and inaccurate way to classify humans biologically. Genetic data for the rejection of biological racial classification comes from the analysis of many genes, including those controlling skin color.

The evolutionary story reinforces the unity of *Homo sapiens*. We all originated from Africa. The genetic variation humans have experienced since migrating out of Africa is extremely limited. We are 99.9 percent genetically identical. The genetic differences we do exhibit are the result of adaptations to the varying environments we encountered as we spread throughout the globe.

Too often, people have tried to exploit human genetic variation by suggesting that the differences they observed offered support for the flawed concept of white supremacy. The sickle cell variant is, perhaps, the best example. Most people carry two normal copies of the gene that encodes the beta chain of the protein hemoglobin. They inherited

---

62. Rosalyn Singleton et al., "Rickets and Vitamin D Deficiency in Alaska Native Children," *Journal of Pediatric Endocrinology and Metabolism* 28, no. 7–8 (July 2015): 815–23, https://doi.org/10.1515/jpem-2014-0446.
63. Ira Gantz, Tadataka Yamada, Takao Tashiro, Yoshitaka Konda, Yoshimasa Shimoto, Hiroto Miwa, Jeffrey M. Trent, "Mapping of the Gene Encoding the Melanocortin-1 (Alpha-Melanocyte Stimulating Hormone) Receptor (MC1R) to Human Chromosome 16q24.3 by Fluorescence *in Situ* Hybridization," *Genomics* 19, no. 2 (January 15, 1994): 394–95, https://doi.org/10.1006/geno.1994.1080.

one from each biological parent. Red blood cells make hemoglobin and use it to carry oxygen in our blood. In parts of the world where malaria is endemic, some people carry a variant of the hemoglobin beta gene: the sickle cell variant. If a person inherits one normal copy of the hemoglobin beta gene and one sickle cell variant, they experience very little reduction in the ability of their red blood cells to carry oxygen and they are resistant to malaria, a deadly disease caused by the parasite *Plasmodium falciparum*. If they carry two copies of the sickle cell variant, they have sickle cell disease. The altered form of hemoglobin beta folds incorrectly, causing misshapen red blood cells to form. These misshapen red blood cells are fragile. They break, leading people with sickle cell disease to experience severe anemia, extreme lethargy, pain, vision problems, edema, and frequent infections. The symptoms of sickle cell anemia, the prevalence among African Americans because their ancestors came from places where malaria was endemic, and the flawed conviction of white supremacist views generated distorted attitudes that people of color were lazy and genetically inferior.

The opinion that people of color were genetically inferior persisted and, sadly, some in the scientific community tried to find biological evidence to support that faulty belief. One trait that was intensely scrutinized was IQ. Scientists performed numerous studies attempting to measure the heritability of intelligence, and some of those scientists tried to link intelligence to race. Arthur Jensen, a professor at the University of California, published a particularly troubling paper in 1969.[64] Jensen argued that differences in performance in school and on intelligence tests

---

64. Arthur R. Jensen, "Intelligence, Learning Ability and Socioeconomic Status," *The Journal of Special Education* 3, no. 1 (January 1, 1969): 23–35, https://doi.org/10.1177/002246696900300103.

between whites and blacks were due more to genetic than to environmental factors. Since the publication of Jensen's controversial paper, countless studies have soundly refuted Jensen's thesis.[65] Stephen Jay Gould summarizes the reaction to Jensen's claim in his essay in *Race and IQ*.

> I merely point out that a specific claim purporting to demonstrate a mean genetic deficiency in the intelligence of American blacks rests upon no new facts whatever and can cite no valid data in its support. It is just as likely that blacks have a genetic advantage over whites. And, either way, it doesn't matter a damn. An individual can't be judged by his group mean.[66]

Attempts to use biology to classify people definitively by skin color, IQ, blood type, or susceptibility to specific diseases or drug efficacy have uniformly failed. Regardless of the failure of biological data to support any division of human beings into separate races, the destructive opinions persisted. Health, inheritance, and ancestry became intimately entangled with economics and politics as people in power made decisions on funding priorities that continued to disadvantage people of color.

Scientists have called for an end to the use of the word *race*.[67] They argue that "the use of biological concepts of race in human genetic research—so disputed and so

---

65. Ashley Montagu, *Race and IQ* (New York: Oxford University Press, 1999); Theodosius Dobzhansky, *Mankind Evolving: The Evolution of the Human Species* (New Haven: Yale University Press, 1962); Theodosius Dobzhansky, *Genetic Diversity and Human Equality* (New York: Basic, 1973); Theodosius Dobzhansky, *Heredity and the Nature of Man* (New York: Harcourt, Brace & World, 1963); B. Devlin, Michael Daniels, and Kathryn Roeder, "The Heritability of IQ," *Nature* 388, no. 6641 (July 31, 1997): 468–71, https://doi.org/10.1038/41319.
66. Montagu, *Race and IQ*, 188–89.
67. Michael Yudell, Dorothy Roberts, Rob DeSalle, and Sarah Tishkoff, "Taking

mired in confusion—is problematic at best and harmful at worst. It is time for biologists to find a better way."[68] They concur with the numerous studies that failed to find a biological basis for race, stating that "racial classifications do not make sense in terms of genetics."[69] Yudell and colleagues point out that ancestry provides useful information because it is a process-based concept. Ancestry provides information about one person's relationship to others in their genealogical history. Race is different. It is a taxonomic notion that depends not on process but on pattern. Race attempts to "draw conclusions about hierarchical organization of humans which connect an individual to a larger preconceived geographically circumscribed or socially constructed group."[70] They propose that scientists avoid the use of the word *race* completely, substituting *ancestry* or *population* instead. "Phrasing out racial terminology in biological sciences would send an important message to scientists and the public alike: Historical racial categories that are treated as natural and infused with notions of superiority and inferiority have no place in biology."[71] The authors fully acknowledge that while race is not real, racism is all too real and that studying racism and its biological and sociological effects are critical.

Evolutionary theory tells us that our connection to all of creation runs deep and reminds us that we are embodied creatures on a journey. Our journey is one in which members of our species have experienced changes in the genes we carry. Sometimes these changes are detrimental. Some-

Race out of Human Genetics," *Science* 351, no. 6273 (February 5, 2016): 564, https://doi.org/10.1126/science.aac4951.
68. Yudell et al., "Taking Race out of Human Genetics," 564.
69. Yudell et al., "Taking Race out of Human Genetics," 565.
70. Yudell et al., "Taking Race out of Human Genetics," 565.
71. Yudell et al., "Taking Race out of Human Genetics," 565.

times the changes are opportunities for adaptation to a new environment. The living organisms around us are on a similar journey. In covenantal relationship with God, our neighbors, and all of creation, God asks us to care for God's beloved creation.

Evolutionary theory connects us to one other in an enormous family tree. Every human can trace his or her roots to Africa. The slight variations in our genomes do not make us more or less than our fellow *Homo sapiens*. They are random changes that might be neutral or may be adaptations that provided an advantage in our ancestors' environments. None of our traits—our skin color, blood type, IQ, cranial shape, or lactose tolerance—can definitively place us into a distinct race and certainly do not determine our worth. We are part of a beautiful continuum of humanity without distinct boundaries. In light of our deep evolutionary connections, it is difficult to avoid wondering what might happen if we all fully embraced this continuum. Would it be easier to see all our fellow human beings as our sisters and brothers? Might we focus more on our extensive similarities rather than our minute differences? Maybe an evolutionary worldview would keep the reality of our embodied relational reality in the forefront of our minds as we care for each other and the world created and loved by God.

On your next bike ride or hike in the woods, join me in observing and celebrating the world around you. Use the encounter with the plants, animals, and people to generate worship of God who created of it all. Consider your relationships with the living organisms around you. *Wow!* Celebrate your similarities and your differences. *Thanks!* Give thanks that you and all species around you are on an evolutionary journey. Finally, *help!* Ask God to remind you of your deep connections to other humans and the created world whenever you make choices about how to live in this beautiful world created by God.

6.

Jesus Can Hit a Curve Ball: What It Means to Be Made in the Image of God

Jason Lief

> The love for all living creatures is the most noble attribute of man.
> —Charles Darwin, *The Descent of Man*

I started playing baseball in grade school on one of the little-league teams. The teams were always sponsored by a local business, and I happened to be on one sponsored by a trucking company—the name was on our jerseys in big red letters. We won the little-league championship that year, but I was terrible. Most of the time I was stuck out in right field, praying the ball wasn't hit to me. At the plate I was just hoping to get walked. My dad would bribe me with Star Wars action figures, but to no avail. I was scared of the ball, so I wasn't swinging the bat. Strike me out or walk me—those were the options. When I picked the game back up in high school, I fared much better. I learned to play first base, I developed into a serviceable junk ball pitcher, and I started to hit. I remember being taught to hammer down on the ball. Coaches would yell at me to hit the top half of the ball, so I did. I batted about .300, and by my senior year I was even hitting home runs.

When I started coaching baseball, I taught what I knew. Swing down, hit the top half of the ball, put it on the ground and beat it out. My teams played good defense, knew where to go with the ball, and even had good pitching, but we couldn't hit. It wasn't until an assistant coach showed me a video on rotational hitting that I began to wonder if my approach to hitting was wrong. Rotational hitting calls for a slight upper cut and keeping your elbow in—the opposite of what every little league dad yells at their kid ("Keep your elbow up!")—and a very small step, mainly using the hips to generate power. With nothing to lose, we began to teach rotational hitting. We changed our language, telling kids to keep their hands back, open the hips, keep their elbow tucked in, and try to hit fly balls. Wouldn't you know, our hitting improved. Our batting average skyrocketed, and by my last year as a varsity coach we won over twenty games.

Our move from linear hitting to rotational hitting is the perfect example of a paradigm shift. Linear hitting, which emphasizes hitting ground balls and hitting the top of the baseball, developed with the popularity of the aluminum bat. It focuses on percentages. Because high-school players are still developing, hitting it on the ground means there is a greater chance of getting on base. It had very little to do with the science or fundamentals of baseball. In fact, most great hitters in the major leagues use rotational hitting. In rotational hitting, the bat stays on the plane of the incoming pitch much longer, increasing the chance of making good contact. The slight uppercut has little to do with hitting home runs or fly balls; it has everything to do with angles and a more natural swing. Give a little kid a bat and tell him or her to swing, and most of the time they naturally use rotational form.

Linear hitting developed because it produced success on the high-school level. By the time I was in high school, it was the accepted way to hit. You'd go to the baseball clinics and everyone taught it; very few coaches questioned it. Which is why some players stubbornly refused to switch to rotational hitting. It sounded strange to them; it went against everything they had been taught about hitting. Some of them had been successful with their own approach, so they were hesitant to change. By the end of the season, everyone had bought in. They saw other players become much better hitters and realized there must be something to it.

This lesson in hitting a baseball provides a metaphor for thinking about the tension in the Christian community over questions of science. For some, believing evolution is true goes against what they've been taught. Many Christian young people have been brought up believing in a literal six-day creation. To read the Bible any other way is to step onto a slippery slope that opens the door to all sorts of ideas. They refuse to consider the scientific evidence because they can't get past the biblical and theological obstacles. All of this leads to an unhealthy refusal to engage in conversations or explore scientific insights. They don't recognize Christians have not always read the Bible this way. Science has changed and developed, forcing communities to rethink their understanding of the cosmos and our place in it. The point isn't to make sure everyone believes the same things; the point is to help them see how we always use language to give expression to our understanding of God and science. Healthy dialogue will only come with a humility that doesn't confuse the living God with doctrinal expressions or conflate the created world with scientific theory. Both are necessary, but both are subject to change. So, what does it look like to help young people develop a language for Christian faith that is open to new insights from scientific inquiry? That's what we'll explore in this chapter.

Poetry and Paradigms

With his book *The Structure of Scientific Revolutions*, Thomas Kuhn challenged the way people thought about scientific progress. Traditionally, it was believed that science moved in a linear fashion, with new ideas adding to what is already known. Progress seemed to be an upward, steady climb. Kuhn, however, suggested that scientific progress wasn't quite so steady and that it wasn't just about adding to prior knowledge. Early forms of scientific inquiry included a variety of perspectives in competition with each other. Kuhn writes, "The early developmental stages of most sciences have been characterized by continual competition between a number of distinct views of nature, each partially derived from, and all roughly compatible with the dictates of scientific observation and method."[1] What made them distinct was their different "ways of seeing the world" and how they practiced science in relation to that worldview.[2] Kuhn describes normal science as the development of a paradigm that represents a common understanding of the cosmos with shared theories and models. The paradigm becomes the default way of exploring new scientific problems, which means that "research is based on shared paradigms . . . committed to the same rules and standards for scientific practice."[3] When paradigms are confronted with anomalies or problems that raise questions about the paradigm, the result can be a crisis that calls the rules of a particular paradigm into question.[4]

---

1. Thomas S. Kuhn, *The Structure of Scientific Revolutions: 50th Anniversary Edition* (Chicago: University of Chicago Press, 2012), 4.
2. Kuhn, *Structure of Scientific Revolutions*, 4.
3. Kuhn, *Structure of Scientific Revolutions*, 11.
4. Kuhn, *Structure of Scientific Revolutions*, 84.

Scientific revolutions are the result of a crisis, which in the end discloses a new paradigm.

Looking backward, it's easy to see moments of scientific revolution. From the Copernican revolution to Einstein's theory of relativity, there are moments when the old paradigm gives way to something new, and a new way of seeing and thinking about the cosmos is born that eventually has an effect upon human culture. Darwin's theory of evolution fits this criterion. The impact of this paradigm shift, from an ordered universe created by a rational god to a theory of biological life based on natural selection, is still working itself out. The tension between science and faith, and the impact on the church, is one effect of this new paradigm. But this isn't the first time a paradigm shift has caused theological problems.

At the time of the Copernican revolution, the Reformers struggled with what it meant for the Christian faith. John Calvin writes,

> The Christian is not to compromise so as to obscure the distinction between good and evil and is to avoid the errors of those dreamers who have a spirit of bitterness and contradiction, who reprove everything and prevent the order of nature. We will see some who are so deranged, not only in religion but who in all things reveal their monstrous nature, that they will say that the sun does not move, and that it is the earth which shifts and turns. When we see such minds we must indeed confess that the devil possesses them, and that God sets them before us as mirrors, in order to keep us in his fear. So, it is with all who argue out of pure malice, and who happily make a show of their imprudence. When they are told: "That is hot," they will reply: "No, it is plainly cold." When they are shown an object that is black, they will say that it is white, or vice versa. Just like the man who said that snow is black; for although it is perceived and known by all to be white, yet he clearly wished to contradict the fact. And so it

is that they are madmen who would try to change the natural order, and even to dazzle eyes and benumb their senses.[5]

Luther also responded negatively to Copernicus, saying, "So it goes now. Whoever wants to be clever . . . must do something of his own. This is what that fellow does who wishes to turn the whole of astronomy upside down. . . . I believe the Holy Scriptures, for Joshua commanded the sun to stand still, and not the earth."[6] For Luther, Calvin, and the theologians of the early church, the philosophical and scientific paradigm shaped the way they read the Bible. Natural science, or natural philosophy as it was called, provided a way of making sense of the world, which influenced the way they thought about God, humanity, and salvation. In fact, the Reformation is part of a philosophical shift that had a profound impact upon science. While Christians from Augustine to Aquinas, to Luther and Calvin were influenced by a particular philosophical and scientific understanding of the world, they were careful to insist that the Bible not be chained to a particular scientific paradigm.

Augustine was explicit about this. In *The Literal Meaning of Genesis* he writes,

> In matters that are so obscure and far beyond our vision, we find in Holy Scripture passages which can be interpreted in very different ways without prejudice to the faith we have received. In such cases, we should not rush in headlong and so firmly take our stand on one side that, if further progress in the search of truth justly undermines this position, we too fall with it. That would be to battle not for the teaching of

---

5. Wyatt Houtz, "John Calvin on Nicolaus Copernicus and Heliocentrism," BioLogos, October 28, 2014, https://tinyurl.com/yad8qwms.
6. Owen Gingerich, "Did the Reformers Reject Copernicus?," *Christianity Today*, https://tinyurl.com/y75qnqtn.

Holy Scripture but for our own, wishing its teaching to conform to ours, whereas we ought to wish ours to conform to that of Sacred Scripture.[7]

Augustine's point is that the Bible should not be strongly linked with a particular scientific paradigm because if that paradigm is proven to be wrong, then our interpretation of the Bible becomes problematic. Calvin advocated for a similar position in his emphasis on accommodation. Here's what Calvin writes in his commentary on the Psalms:

> Moses calls the sun and moon the two great lights, and there is little doubt that the Psalmist here borrows the same phraseology. What is immediately added about the stars, is, as it were, accessory to the others. It is true, that the other planets are larger than the moon, but it is stated as second in order on account of its visible effects. The Holy Spirit had no intention to teach astronomy; and, in proposing instruction meant to be common to the simplest and most uneducated persons, he made use by Moses and the other Prophets of popular language, that none might shelter himself under the pretext of obscurity, as we will see men sometimes very readily pretend an incapacity to understand, when anything deep or recondite is submitted to their notice. Accordingly, as Saturn though bigger than the moon is not so to the eye owing to its greater distance, the Holy Spirit would rather speak childishly than unintelligibly to the humble and unlearned.[8]

While Luther and Calvin struggled to make sense of the scientific changes taking place in their own day, their theological approach to interpreting the Bible allowed for, and even encouraged, the exploration of the cosmos through

---

7. Cited in Tim Reddish, *Science and Christianity: Foundations and Frameworks for Moving Forward in Faith* (Eugene, OR: Wipf & Stock, 2016), 4.
8. Cited in Houtz, "John Calvin," https://tinyurl.com/yad8qwms.

science. Calvin's emphasis on accommodation made space for the Bible to be read as the truth about God and God's work of salvation in Jesus Christ without being undermined by every new scientific discovery.

New philosophical and scientific paradigms did, however, change the way people thought about faith. While Christians ground their ideas of God in the Bible, these ideas are always mediated through language. Language shapes the way we think about the world, and it provides a way of thinking about God. In the same way science changes with the development of new paradigms, so too biblical and theological interpretation changes as language and culture change. This isn't the radical postmodern relativism that Sunday-school teachers warn about; it is merely the recognition that language shapes the way human beings see the world. Just like the natural sciences, theology, as a science, has paradigms. We develop ways of interpreting the Bible and talking about God that make sense within a particular culture. The problem is many people don't think of their interpretation of the Bible as a paradigm; they think of it as the absolute truth about God and the world. So, when other Christians provide a different interpretation, conflict arises. When everyone sees their interpretation as Truth (with a capital T), it makes it hard to have meaningful conversation.

When the faith and science discussion focuses on Genesis, it often fails to recognize the deeper issues of interpretation, language, and paradigms. Arguing about the length of days in Genesis 1, the meaning of the Hebrew word for day, the historicity of Adam and Eve, or whether snakes could talk before the fall are important conversations, but they rarely get us anywhere. This is because these conversations depend on how we read and interpret the Bible, which flow out of definitions of truth, language, and philosophy. I remember having a debate with someone over a particular cultural issue that led us back to the opening chapters of Genesis. Ultimately, our dialogue reached a stalemate—an agree-to-disagree moment—when it became apparent that we read the Genesis creation stories differently based upon different approaches to interpretation and truth. Like dominos falling in different directions, this starting point usually leads down different and irreconcilable paths.

Not that beginning with the incarnation eliminates all questions about interpretation and truth; it does, however, ground the discussion in the central claim of the Christian faith—the revelation of God in Jesus Christ. Starting here avoids the polarizing issues in Genesis by pushing us toward a biblical and theological conversation about what it means to say God became human. The Bible uses multiple metaphors, which has allowed theologians throughout the history of the church to develop different theological models for talking about the incarnation and salvation. While some models are privileged over others at particular historical moments, no one says all the others are wrong. As a result, Christianity has been able to adapt to a variety of cultures without losing the central thrust of the gospel. Similarly, Christian faith has always been able to adapt to different scientific paradigms without losing the central message of the gospel.

Jesus Meets Darwin

In her book *Christ in Evolution*, Ilia Delio gives a short history of how the church has interpreted the incarnation. She insists that our understanding of the incarnation is always "shaped by a particular theology, philosophy, social and political climate."[9] In other words, the very meaning of the incarnation is that God entered into the historical and cultural experience of humans. Therefore, we can only make sense of the incarnation through cultural expression even as we are careful to recognize the concepts and language we use never exhaust the identity of God in Jesus Christ.

In the premodern world, Christians made sense of the incarnation using Greek and Ptolemaic categories that gave order and meaning to their human experience. Early Christian communities used these cultural tools to give expression to their beliefs about God and humanity, and how God is at work in the world in Jesus Christ. These expressions established essential biblical and theological truths. However, an important question for the Western church today is: What happens when these ancient philosophical and scientific categories no longer make sense? I'm not saying we should get rid of the creeds and doctrines they developed; they must, however, be interpreted for a new historical and cultural moment, which includes new scientific paradigms.

Ilia Delio provides an example of what it looks like when Christian faith is interpreted in a new historical and scientific context. She does this by asking whether neo-Darwinism provides a way of speaking about the world that is compatible with Christianity and the incarnation. She writes, "Thus we can say, according to neo-Darwinian science, evolution is a self-organizing process with an overall increase in adaptive complexity, despite periods of critical instabilities and catastrophes. The process of evolution exhibits a dynamic pattern of 'crisis and renewal' . . . which gives rise to new, more organized and more inclusive forms of life."[10] For Delio, the languages of evolution and Christian faith are compatible if we take the time to

---

9. Ilia Delio, *Christ in Evolution* (Maryknoll, NY: Orbis, 2008), 29.
10. Delio, *Christ in Evolution*, 19.

bring them into conversation. This is not to say we should impose the evolutionary framework on the Bible or theology—this is not what Delio does. Her work is an example of a transversal approach in that it demonstrates how the pattern of creation and new creation found in Scripture is compatible with an evolutionary interpretation of created life.

The nature of this conversation is critical dialogue. Too often the Christian community wants a one-way conversation, imposing what they think are biblical and theological truths onto science. Unfortunately, these truths are more often culturally conditioned categories. Our purpose is to see how theology and evolution can inform each other, correct each other, and in the process deepen what we can learn about God and the created world. Through this deepening, I believe the Christian community can gain insight into human identity and the struggle for meaning that can have a positive impact on how we do pastoral care. While this insight has a wide range of applications, our focus will be to explore the impact it has for young people living in the West. How might a dialogue between faith and science open up new insights into youth ministry? To get started, I return to Paul and his view of the incarnation found in Colossians.

From Death to New Life

An important theme in Paul's letters is the movement from an old way of life to something new. In Romans, this gets expressed as the move from Adam to Christ. Paul summarizes this by saying, "So you also must consider yourselves dead to sin and alive to God in Christ Jesus" (Rom 6:11). An important part of this transformation is the way in which Paul sees the death and resurrection of Jesus Christ as the foundation for a new life free from the oppressive cultural categories and labels used to name and divide people. In his letter to the Galatians, Paul is upset because the Christian community is turning back to the old way of life governed by "elemental spirits." He says that faith transforms those who believe from "slaves" to "children" who are "clothed with Christ." He goes on to say, "There is no longer Jew or Greek, there is no longer slave or free, there is no longer male and female; for all of you are one in Christ Jesus" (Gal 3:28). At the heart of Paul's gospel message is the revelation of God's love for humanity in the incarnation of Jesus Christ. In Jesus Christ, God reveals a way of life that is not governed by abstract principles; it is instead a new way of being in the world grounded in love and grace. This eschatological impulse in which the death and resurrection of Christ frees humanity from the old way of life to the new is at the heart of Paul's letters. The cross puts the old to death, making possible something new.

This message is also at the heart of Paul's letter to the Colossians:

> See to it that no one takes you captive through philosophy and empty deceit, according to human tradition, according to the elemental spirits of the universe, and not according to Christ. For in him the whole fullness of deity dwells bodily, and you have come to fullness in him, who is the head of every ruler and authority. In him also you were circumcised with a spiritual circumcision, by putting off the body of the flesh in the circumcision of Christ; when you were buried with him in baptism, you were also raised with him through faith in the power of God, who raised him from the dead. And when you were dead in trespasses and the uncircumcision of your flesh, God made you alive together with him, when he forgave us all our trespasses, erasing the record that stood against us with its legal demands. He set

this aside, nailing it to the cross. He disarmed the rulers and authorities and made a public example of them, triumphing over them in it. Therefore do not let anyone condemn you in matters of food and drink or of observing festivals, new moons, or sabbaths. These are only a shadow of what is to come, but the substance belongs to Christ. Do not let anyone disqualify you, insisting on self-abasement and worship of angels, dwelling on visions, puffed up without cause by a human way of thinking, and not holding fast to the head, from whom the whole body, nourished and held together by its ligaments and sinews, grows with a growth that is from God. (Col 2:8–19)

The old way of life is one in which the social and cultural patterns determines what it means to be human. In the case of the Colossian people, it was a culture where the emperors were divine, and temples and shrines were built to them. What's more important is how the patterns of creation were deified, invested with more power and authority then they possessed.

This is the context in which Paul reminds them of the power of Christ's death and resurrection. He tells them to not be taken captive, that they have been spiritually circumcised—baptized into Christ's death and resurrection. This old way of life, this twisted, misdirected way of life, is put to death. On the cross, God breaks us down in order to bring forth a new form of humanity capable of loving God and loving our neighbor. This is what Paul tells them: "God made you alive together with him" by disarming "the rulers and authorities and made a public spectacle of them, triumphing over them in it." One way to think about this is that on the cross Jesus frees the world to be the world. On the cross of Christ, God makes possible a new future, freeing humanity and creation from the past so they might become something new. According to Paul, cultural and religious ideologies are insufficient pictures of the world. Traditions that attempt to merely maintain the status quo or preserve a particular ordering of the world are shown to be demonic. Paul says that Christ has disarmed them, he has made a public spectacle of them, he has blown open every human attempt to say, "This is the truth about the world."

For Paul, the death and resurrection of Jesus Christ has unmasked the inwardly turned world of the Colossian people. He challenges the emperor and the use of fear and violence to maintain power. Paul takes on the hierarchical patterns that valued some and saw others as worthless. He warns them not to give in to these old patterns. Like Abraham and Israel before them, they have been called out. In Christ, God has freed them to live as God's people. They are no longer held captive by dietary laws or festivals, religious or secular; Paul is saying to them these patterns and practices no longer determine their identity. He reminds them that their identity is grounded only in Jesus Christ. Paul reminds them that on the cross God has killed the old humanity, which has been replaced by the new humanity in Christ. They are now a part of the body—the new humanity—in Jesus Christ. In Christ they have died to the elemental spirits; the old way of life no longer has any power. The death of Christ and his resurrection free us for a new way of being human in the world, a new way that is grounded in our future, in the revelation of our future in the resurrection.

Paul wants the Colossian people to see how the death and resurrection of Jesus Christ shapes the pattern of the biblical story. In Genesis, God brings forth the possibility of life out of the darkness and chaos of the primordial waters. "The earth was a formless void and darkness covered the face of the deep." The act of creation is always a movement from darkness to light, from chaos to order, in which God brings forth the conditions necessary for life. In the exodus event, God once again brings forth the possibility for new life out of the darkness and death (plagues nine and ten) by freeing the Israelites from Egypt and bringing them into the promised land. The incarnation of God in Jesus Christ, his ministry, his death, and his resurrection are the fulfillment of this movement. Out of darkness and death comes the revelation of new life, freeing us from the old way of life and leading us into a new way of being human.

This pattern—from death to life, old to new, chaos to order—finds resonance with the scientific insights of a neo-Darwinist perspective. The Christian community only has to have the courage and the imagination to see it. The only way this happens is by being willing to engage in the conversation. This means taking biblical and theological interpretation seriously, engaging the deeper questions of language, context, and meaning; it means being willing to read the Bible in a transhistorical or transcultural way, refusing to lock the message of Scripture into an ancient cosmology, and being willing to seriously consider the insights that might be gained from contemporary scientific perspectives.

Rather than beginning with a hyperliteral interpretation of Genesis that boxes the reader into a particular understanding of Jesus Christ and God's work of salvation, starting with the incarnation opens us to the message of the gospel not just for humanity but for all of creation. Rather than see the creation as a static given in which the drama unfolds, we are able to see the deep connections between creation and incarnation. When we recognize that the Christians of earlier times were wrestling with the meaning of the gospel within the context of a different worldview, one that viewed the spiritual and the material in a vertical way, we can see how their scientific and philosophical perspectives shaped the way they did theology as they interpreted the revelation of God in Jesus Christ. This doesn't mean their ideas are bad, or that they should be discarded; it does mean that they have to be interpreted into an entirely new way of making sense of the cosmos.

Back to the Future: The Promise of Creation

The dramatic cultural and philosophical changes that led to the Reformation provided a new way of thinking about the incarnation and Christ's work of salvation—what can be called an eschatological way of thinking. The relationship between the spiritual and the material is no longer a vertical relationship; it is also horizontal. Jesus Christ is not just the Son who comes from above (although he is that); he is also the resurrected Christ who comes from the future to open the possibility of a new way of life. This eschatological view of the incarnation makes possible an interpretation of creation that is open to a new future, providing a new way for the Christian community to approach scientific inquiry.

This eschatological approach can be found in the theology of John Calvin. In *Calvin's Doctrine of Man*, T. F. Torrance describes Calvin's belief in God's continuous creation. Appealing to Calvin's commentary on the Psalms, Torrance describes how God always brings new life out of nothing. He quotes Calvin as saying, "The world is daily renewed, because God sends forth his Spirit. In this propagation of living creatures we doubtlessly see continually a new creation of the world. . . . All the deaths which take place among living creatures are just so many examples of our nothingness, so to speak; and when others are produced and grow up in their room, we have in that presented to us a renewal of the world."[11]

Turning to humanity, Torrance finds a "dynamic view of the relation of man and God" in Calvin's thought, in which the "image of God" is the development of the relationship between God and humanity. Torrance writes,

> Therefore our life is but an "empty image" unless we keep close to God. When we do we become a "vital life." There can be no doubt that Calvin lays the stress therefore on the dynamic character of the image of God which is maintained in man by continuous conformity to God, by continuous obedience to the claim of the divine will upon him. In other words, the *imago dei* is interpreted teleologically as above and beyond man in terms of man's destiny which is made known in the Word of God, and in the claim of the divine will this revealed upon man's life.[12]

The incarnation of God in Jesus Christ is the fulfillment of the creation as it moves through death and suffering into a promised future. This means that creation is never static; it is always on the way. This understanding of human identity affirms the temporal life; it affirms the processes of change and becoming that are central to evolution. Far from negating the meaning of humanity or the moral good, as some religious opponents of evolution suggest, we discover a theological language that takes evolutionary theory and embodied human life seriously, grounding them in the revelation of God and humanity in Jesus Christ.

German theologian Wolfhart Pannenberg takes this eschatological interpretation further by describing the meaning of creation as sharing "in the life of God." This

---

11. Thomas F. Torrance, *Calvin's Doctrine of Man* (Eugene, OR: Wipf & Stock, 1997), 62.
12. Torrance, *Calvin's Doctrine of Man*, 65.

is only possible when creation participates in the "eschatological future of the resurrection of the dead, which has already come in Jesus Christ." Creation does not find its meaning in some finished, static, "beginning." Instead, all of creation finds its meaning in the eschatological future revealed in the resurrection of Jesus Christ.

This can be seen in Pannenberg's understanding of what it means to be made in the "image of God." The Christian community tends to see the image of God as something given in the past. Because of the fall, this image has either been lost or badly broken, in need of restoration or repair. Salvation, in this context, is about restoration, which means the incarnation is a response to human sin. But this also means that our humanity is grounded in a past static image that opens the door to a form of natural law that determines what it means to be human. The problem with natural law is that it's conservative in a bad way; it wants to keep things the same. It also causes people to assume that the culture they live in is *the* way human beings are supposed to live. Change, for the most part, is bad. If human identity is something given in the past, then change is negative—a distortion of what we were created to be. This, in turn, affirms the social and cultural status quo.

Pannenberg believes our true human identity is revealed in Jesus Christ. He writes, "In the story of the human race, then, the image of God was not achieved fully at the outset. It was still in process. This is true not only of the likeness but of the image itself. . . . This full actualization is our destiny, one that was historically achieved with Jesus Christ and in which others may participate by transformation into the image of Christ."[13] In this way, the incarnation is not only a response to the fall; it is the fulfillment—the

---

13. Wolfhart Pannenberg, *Anthropology in Theological Perspective*, trans. Matthew J. O'Connell (New York: T&T Clark, 2004), 217.

destiny—of all creation. The resurrection of Jesus Christ is the fulfillment of what it means to be the "image of God." Pannenberg writes, "Therefore the incarnation cannot be an external appendix to creation nor a mere reaction of the Creator to Adam's sin. From the very first it is the crown of God's world order, the supreme concentration of the active presence of the Logos in creation."[14]

Pannenberg believes human identity comes from outside of our self—what he refers to as exocentricity or openness to the world. This means that human identity is given to us by God, revealed in Jesus Christ. At the same time, our human identity is deeply connected with our relationships to the creation. Our humanity must never be reduced to abstract forms of spirituality; it is always connected to our life as embodied souls in relationship with creation. Because our identity comes from outside of us, our true identity is bound up in our relationships. For Pannenberg, to know God is to know Jesus Christ. Similarly, to know what it means to be human is to know Jesus Christ. Christ is the center of human existence, revealing our humanity in relation to God and the created world. This is why Christ has to be at the center of science. Not in a fundamentalist way, making science fit into a literal reading of the Bible, but in a way that sees how science is connected to God's love for creation revealed in the incarnation. This allows Christians to courageously explore the world through science, knowing that Christ is at the center of it all.

In a similar way, theologian Jürgen Moltmann views creation as an open process that moves into a promised future. An important part of this, for Moltmann, is creation's movement toward embodiment. He writes,

---

14. Wolfhart Pannenberg, *Systematic Theology Volume 2* (Grand Rapids: Eerdmans, 1994), 64.

> According to the biblical traditions, embodiment is the end of God's works in creation. The earth is the object and the scene of the Creator's fertile and inventive love. It was bodily, sensuous human beings whom he created to be his image, and his first commandment was "Be fruitful and multiply" . . . (Gen. 1.28). It is not the spirituality of men and women, and not what distinguishes them from animals, which makes them God's image on earth. They are his image in their whole and particular bodily existence. . . . Embodiment is his goal. All the paths of his spirit and all the worlds of his speech end in the lived form and configuration of his body.[15]

The incarnation, for Moltmann, is not primarily a response to human sin, even though God deals with sin through the death and resurrection of Jesus Christ. The incarnation is the prism through which we discover the meaning of creation. For Moltmann, the resurrection of Jesus Christ is not just the undoing of the fall, it is the consummation of creation "in the beginning"—the promise of a new future that flows from its relationship with God.

Taken together, Delio, Pannenberg, and Moltmann offer important theological insights on the relationship between faith and science. While they are faithful to the biblical testimony, they interpret the death and resurrection of Jesus Christ within a contemporary frame, which makes it possible to engage in a dialogue with contemporary scientific paradigms. The theological pattern is one that moves from darkness and death to new life, which, as Elizabeth Johnson and Ilia Delio show us, is the pattern of evolution. What happens when we bring theology and evolution into dialogue? How does evolution change the way we talk about God?

---

15. Jürgen Moltmann, *God in Creation: A New Theology of Creation and the Spirit of God* (Minneapolis: Fortress Press, 1993), 245.

Evolution and God's Love

The tendency in evangelical Christianity is to see the doctrine of creation as a demonstration of the power of God. God is viewed as a king, as a sovereign, who rules and governs the creation. This lends itself to traditional views of salvation in which there must be punishment for sin, or some form of satisfaction must be made. God heroically comes to take the wrath upon God's self, taking our place to bear the punishment for sin, so humanity can be reconciled and so everything can be put back in right order.

It's easy to see how this view comes into conflict with evolution. If God is the sovereign King, then the natural world has to have order, it has to have a grand plan, it has to have a designer. This is seen in the language of the Christian community that often wants to point to design and order in the creation as proof for the existence of God. Historically, this type of argument, known as the cosmological argument, focuses on principles like causation, order, and intelligence to make the case for God and faith. It's easy to see how evolution causes problems for Christians in this context, because Darwin's evolution doesn't need a grand designer or grand plan; it doesn't need an all-powerful God to account for natural life, or even the life of human beings.

But what if the problem isn't Darwin or evolution? What if the problem is our view of God? In *Ask the Beasts: Darwin and the God of Love*, Elizabeth Johnson brings Darwin and evolution into conversation with a biblical and theological view of God as love. She provides a Trinitarian framework for reading the biblical revelation of God as the creator of life. She reminds us how the Nicene creed speaks of the Holy Spirit as the "Lord and giver of life," at work constantly bringing forth new life.[16] She refers to the communal life of the Trinity, a life in which the three persons indwell one another, united in a powerful love that brings forth new life. Like the other theologians discussed in this book, Johnson does not see the incarnation as primarily a response to sin; in the vein of the Franciscan tradition, she speaks of the incarnation as an outworking of divine love. She writes,

> The chain of reasoning of this alternative position has to do with the dynamic of love. God is unfathomable love; love seeks union with the beloved; this union occurs in the incarnation when the divine Word enters into personal union with the created world in Jesus Christ. As a matter of fact, however, human beings did sin, setting up the antagonistic conditions in which Jesus' life ended in suffering and agonizing death. In this way divine love showed itself capable of going all the way into the depths of degradation in order to heal from within. But the incarnation is not dependent on the sin of our first parents. It was Love's very intent from the beginning.[17]

Shifting our view of God from an authoritarian, monarchal view to a much more biblical Trinitarian view of God reveals the truth about God's love for the creation. A theology that focuses on power and control, or divine will and causation, will lead to a view of science that insists on order, causation, and design. The intrusion of sin, suffering, and death into creation is problematic and must be dealt with in a way that satisfies this particular view of God. A view of the created world that allows for change, adaptation, and even death does not fit this picture of God. A different understanding of God, grounded in the Trinitarian

---

16. Elizabeth A. Johnson, *Ask the Beasts: Darwin and the God of Love* (London: Bloomsbury, 2014), 128.
17. Johnson, *Ask the Beasts*, 226.

understanding of God as love, allows for an evolutionary perspective. True love is an act that allows for change; it allows for adaptation. It is a view of God in which God allows the creation to have a life of its own, to develop and adapt, to "struggle for life." True love always opens itself up to the possibility of suffering. In this context, sin, suffering, and even death have a place, not necessarily as God's design or God's plan, but as a part of the beautiful risk that love entails. It is a view of God in which God creates space for the creation, for humanity, to develop. God is less monarch and more an artist who is not in a hurry but knows true beauty takes patience. In this paradigm, God loves the material world and all the processes unleashed when the word was spoken in the beginning. It is a theology that declares God loves humans because we are creatures made from the dust, the same as apes, dogs, and cattle. God loves humans because we come from the water and the land through the beautiful mystery of life made possible by the Holy Spirit at work in this world.

This view of God and God's relationship with the creation is eschatological. This means we are no longer defined by our past. Our identity is not found in some glorified prefall state we are trying to get back to; instead, God calls us into something new. This is the meaning of evangelism and ministry—inviting young people to find their identity in the future that God opens for them in Jesus Christ. This, for Johnson, is the meaning of Christ's death and resurrection. She writes,

> The living God is the future of the world. Time is still stamped with the suffering of Good Friday; days still wander in the silence and loss of Holy Saturday. Yet in wordless expectation, all earthly reality is in tremendous movement toward its own glory which has already arrived by the power of the Spirit in the risen Christ. Put another way, Christ car-

ries the whole creation toward its destiny. His resurrection is the beginning of the resurrection of all flesh. Or so Christians hope. They hope that when the last day does come, it will be nothing less than the "universal Easter of the cosmos".[18]

The medieval mystic Julian of Norwich expressed a similar view of the relationship between God and creation. She wrestled with the same questions that contemporary people wrestle with—the existence of evil and suffering, the source of meaning, and whether or not, if God exists, God is good. Her visions came during a time of intense illness and suffering in which she gazed upon the crucifix, undoubtedly receiving the last rites. During this time, she had a vision of Jesus Christ and his own suffering that opened a different experience of God. Though Julian made sure her teachings were in line with official teachings of the church, her understanding of evil, sin, and God's love moved away from expressions of power and authority. Her visions were an expression of divine love, showing that everything that exists does so because of God's love. Far from satisfying some form of divine wrath or justice, Julian sees in the suffering and death of Jesus Christ God's intense love for creation. Julian writes,

> Then our good Lord Jesus Christ spoke, asking "Are you well pleased that is suffered for you?" I said "Yes, my good Lord, thank you. Yes, my good Lord, blessed may you be!" Then Jesus, our kind Lord, said "If you are pleased, I am pleased. It is a joy, a delight and an endless happiness to me that I ever endured suffering for you, and if I could suffer more, I would suffer more." . . . And if he had died, or was going to die, so often, he would still think nothing of it out of love. For his love is so great that everything seems a trifle to him in comparison . . . for the Passion was a noble, glorious

---

18. Johnson, *Ask the Beasts*, 227.

deed performed at one particular time through the action of love, love whit has always existed and will never end.[19]

Through her visions, Julian came to see the deep relationship between love and suffering. In Jesus Christ, God suffers and dies for us because God loves us. The cross, for Julian, is not primarily an act of punishment that satisfies some form of divine justice; the cross is an expression of God's love that becomes the catalyst for the new creation. She recognizes that the love that drove Jesus Christ to the cross is a love that has always existed; it is the very love that brought forth the creation. This is emphasized in another vision, in which Julian is shown a hazelnut in the palm of her hand. She writes, "I looked at it with my mind's eye and thought, 'What can this be?' And the answer came to me, 'It is all that is made.' I wondered how it could last, for it was so small I thought I might suddenly have disappeared. And the answer in any mind was, 'It lasts and will last forever because God loves it; and everything exists in the same way by the love of God.'"[20]

Julian helps us see the connection between love and suffering. It is the love of God that brings creation into existence, calling it into a new future. It is in this same love that God takes on human flesh in the person of Jesus Christ, not as a plan B, but as an expression of God's love for humanity and all creation. An important part of this expression of love is the death and resurrection of Jesus Christ, suffering and death that brings forth new life, calling humanity and creation into a new future. Julian provides a framework for the Christian community to think differently about the relationship between God and creation, and therefore to

---

19. Julian of Norwich, *Revelations of Divine Love* (Oxford: Oxford University Press, 2015), 72–74.
20. Julian, *Revelations of Divine Love*, 47.

think differently about the findings of science. The hazelnut symbolizes the promise of becoming. Evolutionary theory provides a scientific picture of a world that is in the process of becoming. That through frailty, through suffering, and even through death, God calls the creation to become something new and glorious. What Julian provides is an example of a point of contact between evolution and Christian faith—what we earlier called transversal space. Recognizing the deep connection between the love of God for the world and God's suffering in Jesus Christ allows us to reflect upon the way in which the very creation itself contains this cruciform mark, that creation is called into a new future by the love of God revealed in Jesus Christ—a love that takes us through the cross, through suffering, into a new creation.

Why This Matters for Youth Ministry

Recognizing the importance of paradigms in science and in theology is an important step in helping young people make sense of their beliefs. Instead of meeting evolution head on, which usually results in conflict and defensive postures, it is more important to help young people see the changes that have taken place in science. It's just as important to help them see how theological language also changes, which changes the way scientific paradigms and theological perspectives interact with each other. Many Christians take their worldview for granted, unable to recognize how they have been shaped by a particular way of seeing the world. Similarly, many Christians take their theological worldview for granted, assuming it is *the* Christian way of reading the Bible and talking about God. Helping young people and adults recognize how our language in both disciplines is conditioned can go a long way in easing the tension that can exist between faith and science.

While this might seem to be a bit heavy for youth ministry, if the Christian community is serious about addressing the issue of young people leaving the church, then it is necessary. The approach we take can make or break how the conversation goes. Starting with their questions is important. In my discussions with young people, it's clear they sometimes feel like they need to give the "right" answer; by this, they usually mean the "answers the adults expect of them." The more permission I give for them to ask questions, the more they begin to wrestle with the possibility that evolution might be true. Helping them see how the worldview of the biblical authors is different from a Western scientific worldview, and that this does not take away from the truth of Scripture, goes a long way in helping young people begin to see how faith and science can talk to each other. Similarly, showing them the variety of theological metaphors the church has used to talk about God, humanity, and salvation in Jesus Christ helps young people see how different perspectives are able to dialogue with evolution. While we should never force students to believe in evolution, it must help them see that it is possible to both have faith and believe evolution is true.

Sometimes, those taking a defensive posture in the church are not providing young people with a biblical Christianity. As Kenda Dean argues in her book *Almost Christian*, the American church tends to replace biblical Christianity with an imposter, one that she and others call Moralistic Therapeutic Deism.[21] This tendency has a significant impact on our young people. It distorts their understanding of God, which influences their understanding of

---

21. Kenda Creasy Dean, *Almost Christian: What the Faith of Our Teenagers Is Telling the American Church* (New York: Oxford University Press, 2010).

what it means to be human. When teaching college freshmen, one of the questions I will often ask students is: What if the point of Christian faith is *not* to die and go to heaven? You can imagine the response: some are upset, some argue with me, some dismiss it as one more example of liberal college professors, but others are intrigued, relieved to be able to ask questions they never felt comfortable asking. Those who dismiss the question are usually students who don't see any connection between Christian faith and the cultural world they live in. They take the cultural world as a given—there's no need to question it, and there's no use in trying to change it. The world is as it is. This creates a split between faith and embodied life, with little interaction between the two. If the point of Christianity is to die and go to heaven, then what does God have to do with science or music or sexuality or anything that has to do with created, cultural life? Sure, the Bible teaches us to be moral, to love others, to spread the gospel, but this doesn't have anything to do with quantum physics or Shakespeare. And it certainly doesn't have anything to do with iPhones, Snapchat, football, or ballet.

Youth ministry has to begin to take the implications and messages of science seriously. Not just as a way to keep people in the church but, more importantly, to help them become comfortable with their lived experience as human animals. Youth ministry needs to begin to help young people become content with being human. Youth ministry must open itself to the message of scientific discovery as a way to help young people become open to the God of the Bible, a God who creates because God loves—a God who became incarnate in the person of Jesus Christ, not just to deal with sin and punishment, but as a sign of God's immense love for this created, material world.

7.

When Darwin Wept: Redeeming Suffering and Death

Sara Sybesma Tolsma

> We have lost the joy of the Household, and the solace of our old age:—she must have known how we loved her; oh that she could now know how deeply, how tenderly we do still and shall ever love her dear joyous face. Blessings on her.
> —Charles Darwin on the death of his daughter, Anne Elizabeth Darwin

A few months ago, I was watching the episode "Islands" of BBC's *Planet Earth II* with friends.[1] The now classic scene in which newly hatched marine iguanas evade predatory snakes had us spellbound. The music, the fact that the snakes outnumbered the iguana by dozens, and a rather natural human wariness when it comes to snakes had all of us rooting for the underdog iguana. One of my friends said, "If there is a God who allows that kind of (explicative) stuff to happen, I don't want any part of it." His comment made me pause and think. How do suffering and death fit into the evolutionary and Christian stories? How can an evolutionary understanding of the role of suffering and death speak into our understanding of God?

---

1. *Planet Earth II*, episode 1, "Islands," produced by Elizabeth White and Michael Gunton, presented by David Attenborough, aired November 6, 2016, on BBC One, https://tinyurl.com/yaojz7tw.

Science, Suffering, and Death

Most people avoid talking about suffering and death. We prefer to talk about life and thriving.[2] Even scientists seem uncomfortable with it; textbooks, scientific journals, and review articles freely discuss predation, herbivory, and parasitism but rarely refer to mortality, death, or suffering.[3] Death, however, is an inseparable part of biological relationships. Every living thing requires an energy source. All animals, some plants and fungi, and many single-celled organisms get that energy by feeding on other organisms. Evolutionary theory makes death difficult to avoid because the fight to survive and reproduce is the basis for biological life. For Christians, evolutionary theory raises important theological questions because "evolutionary history is larded with struggle, impermanence, imperfection, and chance."[4] Moreover, it is filled with death. Understanding that we are part of this evolutionary story leads us to wonder about the role of God in this process and whether we can find meaning and purpose in it. Holmes Rolston III speaks to biologists' avoidance of the difficult philosophical and theological questions of death and suffering that evolutionary theory raises:

> Biology in the last half-century has not been particularly comfortable with the word "struggle" which has largely disappeared from biology texts, being replaced by the notions

---

2. Deborah P. Waldrop, "Denying and Defying Death: The Culture of Dying in 21st Century America," *The Gerontologist* 51, no. 4 (August 1, 2011): 571–76, https://doi.org/10.1093/geront/gnr076.
3. Alison N. P. Stevens, "Predation, Herbivory, and Parasitism," *Nature Education Knowledge* 3, no. 10 (2010): 36, https://tinyurl.com/kkmwnzo.
4. Elizabeth A. Johnson, *Ask the Beasts: Darwin and the God of Love* (London: Bloomsbury, 2014), 29.

of "adaptedness" and "fittedness." Still plenty of "struggle" remains in biology (although the switch in emphasis is revealing), and when philosophical participants find that they themselves have ascended via this struggle, they are confronted with the question whether such a struggle can be meaningful.[5]

Christians concerned with creation care rightly emphasize the goodness of creation declared by God in the creation narratives of Genesis. They show how the authors of the Psalms speak about God's love and care for creation poetically. They also point out how we have failed to properly care for the good creation that God loves.[6] There are some who call for us to embrace the pain and death in creation as an essential part of its goodness of creation. This tends to come from an ecological understanding of death and suffering, moving away from a view that sees it only as a consequence of sin.[7] From an ecological perspective, death and life are inextricably intertwined—life cannot exist without death. Let's unpack this a bit and explore what it all means for youth ministry.

What Ecology and Evolution Can Tell Us about Suffering and Death in Creation

Like my friends who watched the marine iguanas with us, my kids loved watching nature television when they were

---

5. Holmes Rolston, *Science and Religion: A Critical Survey* (Philadelphia: Templeton, 2011), 133–34.
6. Steven Bouma-Prediger, *For the Beauty of the Earth: A Christian Vision for Creation Care* (Grand Rapids: Baker Academic, 2010).
7. Keith B. Miller, "'And God Saw That It Was Good': Death and Pain in the Created Order," *Perspectives on Science and Christian Faith* 63, no. 2 (June 2011): 85, https://tinyurl.com/yc9288u6.

young. Our whole family would sit, spellbound, for hours on weekends or a snow day watching with our eyes partly closed. In a typical scene, an African Cape Buffalo separates from its herd. A pride of lions spies the vulnerable buffalo, and a suspenseful chase (with accompanying dramatic music) follows. After several near misses, the brutal lions finally bring down the poor buffalo, struggling to the very end. The scene inevitably caused our young children to cheer for the poor prey animal and sometimes weep when the predator was successful. I reminded them that lions need to eat, and they need to feed their young cubs. The death of the buffalo is nourishment for the lions and allows them to survive. It was a biological and theological lesson for us. Death shapes ecosystems in complex ways. The complexity goes beyond a pride of lions killing and eating a buffalo. The buffalo is a predator of sorts itself. African Cape Buffalo feed on grass and, because they travel and feed in large herds, can wreak havoc on the grass population. If the buffalo population gets too large, grasses are at risk. Buffalo deaths from predatory lions prevent buffalo numbers from achieving or exceeding carrying capacity and indirectly ensure life for the vegetation the buffalo eat. Out of the death of buffalo comes not only nourishment for the lions but also the possibility of flourishing for the grasses, which in turn sustain the long-term viability of the buffalo.

Ecologists have long understood how physical disturbances, such as fire, shape almost all land ecosystems. Fire is destructive, but for the prairie, fire is essential. So are grazing herbivores. Both grazing herbivores and fire kill organisms in a prairie ecosystem as they also open up the possibility for new life. As bison or deer graze, their mouths and hoofs munch and tear at the established prairie plants, opening up areas in the soil for new seeds to germinate. The prairie itself goes through cycles of death and life that need a physical disturbance for restoration. Plants grow and die with the seasons, and over time, dense thatch accumulates. The thatch makes it difficult for new shoots to reach up and capture sunlight through the barrier of plant detritus. Existing plants are smothered, and the dead plant debris impedes their growth. The thatch also insulates the soil, keeping it cold late into spring, slowing new seed germination. The weakening vegetation opens the possibility for opportunistic woody plants to invade the prairie. The trees shade the prairie grasses, making it increasingly difficult for native plants to thrive. The answer to this cycle of death and weakening is fire. Fires destroy invasive woody plants, reopening space for native grasses to flourish. Fires release organic matter from dead plants that can be used immediately rather than in the months or years it would take to decay. Sunlight quickly warms the fire-blackened soil so seeds can germinate. Finally, the seeds of some plants, such as big bluestem, have a higher germination rate after burning and are some of the first plants to reestablish themselves after a prairie fire.[8] Without the disruptive and deadly force of fire, healthy prairie ecosystems could not exist.

One of the ways ecologists study death in ecological systems is by studying the relationships between predators and their prey.[9] A classic predator-prey study is the relationship between the snowshoe hare (*Lepus americanus*) and the Canadian lynx (*Lynx canadensis*) in the boreal region of

---

8. Sherry R. Rohn and Thomas B. Bragg, "Effect of Burning on Germination of Tallgrass Prairie Plant Species," *Proceedings of the North American Prairie Conferences*, January 1, 1989, https://tinyurl.com/y74cmto9.
9. Alan A. Berryman, "The Origins and Evolution of Predator-Prey Theory," *Ecology* 73, no. 5 (October 1992): 1530–35, https://doi.org/10.2307/1940005.

Canada. Scientists have been studying this relationship for more than one hundred years, beginning with an analysis of the Hudson's Bay Company fur-trading records.[10] The snowshoe hare and the lynx exhibit repetitive ten-year coupled predator-prey cycles in which the numbers of lynx rise and fall, mirroring increases and decreases in snowshoe hare numbers, albeit with a slight lag.[11] The simplest explanation for this cycle is that populations of hares increase in the absence of large numbers of predators. Since the lynx is a specialist predator of snowshoe hares, lynx populations also increase, following just behind hare numbers as food (hares) become more abundant. As lynx numbers rise, their increased predation decreases the number of hares. The hare population numbers fall, followed by a decrease in lynx numbers as their food (hares) becomes less plentiful.[12] When lynx numbers decline, the cycle begins anew. This story gets more complex when we take into consideration the availability of a food source for the snowshoe hares, other predators, weather, and social interactions.[13]

Another predator-prey cycle that scientists have studied in detail is the relationship between moose and wolves on

---

10. Charles J. Krebs, Rudy Boonstra, Stan Boutin, and A. R. E. Sinclair, "What Drives the 10-Year Cycle of Snowshoe Hares?," *BioScience* 51, no. 1 (January 1, 2001): 25–35, https://tinyurl.com/y8tdd7od.
11. Duncan Alexander MacLulich, *Fluctuations in the Numbers of Varying Hare (Lepus americanus)* (Toronto: University of Toronto Press, 1937); Nils Chr. Stenseth, Wilhelm Falck, Ottar N. Bjørnstad, and Charles J. Krebs, "Population Regulation in Snowshoe Hare and Canadian Lynx: Asymmetric Food Web Configurations between Hare and Lynx," *Proceedings of the National Academy of Sciences* 94, no. 10 (May 13, 1997): 5147, https://doi.org/10.1073/pnas.94.10.5147.
12. Krebs et al., "What Drives the 10-Year Cycle?"
13. Stenseth et al., "Population Regulation"; Krebs et al., "What Drives the 10-Year Cycle?"

Isle Royale.[14] Isle Royale is an island in Lake Superior approximately fifteen miles from the mainland, near Thunder Bay. Scientists have observed the moose and wolves on this island for fifty years. In this study, the island's isolation keeps the populations of moose and wolves controlled almost entirely by the predator-prey relationship between these two species alone. Little immigration or emigration occurs. Moose were the first large mammal species to arrive on the island around the turn of the century. Until the 1940s, moose population numbers rose and fell depending on food abundance and weather conditions. In the 1940s, wolves came to the island from Canada across an ice bridge that formed with the mainland. Durward Allen began observing the animals shortly thereafter, and scientists have been following the two species on this island ever since.[15] Initially the wolves flourished while moose population growth flattened. The wolves had stumbled upon an abundant food source. A decline in wolves in the mid-1960s was followed by an increase in moose following a pattern scientists saw with the lynx and hare study, presumably due to the abundance or scarcity of predators or prey. Wolf number recovered as food (moose) became more abundant. During the 1970s, wolf population numbers stayed high while the moose population steadily declined. In 1980, factors independent of a strict predator-prey relationship affected the animals on the island. Canine parvovirus, introduced unintentionally by humans, caused the wolf population to plummet. As expected, a steady increase in the population of moose followed the dramatic decrease in predator numbers. The wolf numbers remained low for several years in spite of an abundant food source, perhaps due to a lack of genetic diversity. The initial wolf

---

14. Wolves and Moose of Isle Royale, http://www.isleroyalewolf.org/.
15. Wolves and Moose of Isle Royale, http://www.isleroyalewolf.org/.

population began with a single female and two males. It is possible that the inevitable inbreeding from such a genetic founder effect was having a negative impact on wolf reproduction and survival. In 1996, the winter was an especially hard one. There was a large outbreak of moose ticks, food became scarce, and moose population numbers rapidly declined. The decline in the numbers of moose put a sharp stop to slowly increasing wolf numbers in the subsequent year, and cyclical population fluctuation followed. More recently, both populations have reached critically low numbers. Warming temperatures due to climate change have made it difficult for moose since they are adapted to cold weather. Rather than foraging for the forty pounds of vegetation they need per day to fatten up for lean winter months, they spend hot days in the water to prevent overheating. Even though the winters have been shorter, the moose do not have the reserves they need to flourish thorough the cold months. The warmer temperatures cause a bloom in tick populations, further stressing the moose. A declining moose population means that food for their predators, wolves, has become scarce, keeping wolf numbers low.

Scientists have learned a lot from observing this unique system of predator-prey interactions. The study confirms that the number of prey, in large part, determines the population size of predators because of food abundance. The study reveals that other factors play important roles in determining population size, including weather and disease, although disease is often also related to population size and food abundance. As scientists followed this ecosystem, they learned that wolves prey on the moose that are least likely to survive. In this way, the wolves cull and strengthen the population that remains. The study confirms ecologists' understanding that predation is a mechanism to avoid exceeding an environment's carrying capacity, thus protecting the region from ecological degradation and maintaining its ability to maximally sustain flourishing populations of both predator and prey. Scientists are curious to see how the story of this predator-prey relationship will end. Will one or both species become extinct at this site? On the other hand, will there be a resurgence in animal numbers? Observers report that only two wolves remain on the island, and the moose population is rapidly expanding in response to this relative lack of predators.[16] Scientists are watching, with interest, to see how the moose population responds to the likely event that it will reach and then exceed carrying capacity soon. What kind of ecological degradation will occur? How quickly will ecological degradation manifest itself in smaller numbers of moose? Will the environment recover from the degradation caused when the moose exceed carrying capacity? If so, how long will the recovery take? In what way will scientists observe that death is necessary for a flourishing ecosystem?

It is tempting to see the death and suffering in creation and cling to a question like the one my friend asked when watching the snakes and the iguana or to fall into the problem of theodicy. An evolutionary perspective plus a theology that sees the incarnation as God's intent from the beginning helps us think about suffering in a new, more hope-filled way. In an evolutionary view of creation in which Christ was present from the beginning, God "freely chooses to create a world of creatures, and out of passionate love freely chooses to embrace these creatures anew in the unpredictable self-giving of the incarnation of the

---

16. Christine Mlot, "Two Wolves Survive in World's Longest Running Predator-Prey Study," Science, April 18, 2017, https://tinyurl.com/yc6ffles; Brandon Champion, "Isle Royale's Exploding Moose Population Could Double in Next 4 Years," MLive.com, April 18, 2017, https://tinyurl.com/y7agvdff.

word."[17] This world of creatures that God loves is filled with death and suffering, but we do not suffer alone. God suffers with us and all of creation. "God does not suffer solely for creation's human emergent. . . . God suffers in, with, and under the creative processes of the cosmos for the healing, the salvation, the transformation, and the liberation of the whole of the cosmos itself."[18] Elizabeth Johnson also describes a God who is in solidarity with those who suffer. She describes a God who consoles and heals us in our suffering: "Knowing that we are not abandoned makes all the difference."[19] Observing the life that comes from death in ecological relationships reminds us of the hope we have in Christ. John Polkinghorne rightly points to the cross and Colossians 1:19–20 as the ultimate solution to the problem of evil, "the only satisfactory conclusion to the matter will come if it is indeed true that 'all shall be well.'"[20]

What Evolution and Cellular Biology Can Tell Us about Suffering and Death

Like ecosystems, organisms require death to flourish. Plants form extensive vascular systems out of cellular death. Cellular death can occur pathologically if a cell does not get adequate oxygen or nutrients or the cell membrane

---

17. Denis Edwards, *Partaking of God: Trinity, Evolution, and Ecology* (Collegeville, MN: Liturgical Press, 2014), 101.
18. Gloria L. Schaab, *The Creative Suffering of the Triune God: An Evolutionary Theology* (New York: Oxford University Press, 2007), 163.
19. Elizabeth A. Johnson, *She Who Is: The Mystery of God in Feminist Theological Discourse* (New York: Crossroad, 1992), 266–67.
20. John C. Polkinghorne, *Science and Providence: God's Interaction with the World* (Philadelphia: Templeton, 2005), 79.

is breached. Pathologic cell death (necrosis) usually elicits an inflammatory response and often results in tissue damage—the collateral damage caused when the body reacts to a threat. Necrotic death is unregulated and does not require energy. The kind of cellular death that is necessary to shape the development and life of animals is not necrotic. The cellular death that is a critical component of organismal life is apoptosis, or programmed cell death. When a cell dies by apoptosis, enzymes called caspases trigger apoptotic events; the cell shrinks in size, DNA condenses, enzymes within the cell become active and fragment the cell's DNA into regularly sized pieces, and finally the cell blebs membrane-bound packages called apoptotic bodies. Apoptotic bodies contain cytoplasm, condensed organelles, and genome fragments. Nearby cells phagocytize and degrade these apoptotic bodies.[21] Apoptotic death does not stimulate an inflammatory response, and the organism avoids the accompanying tissue damage that often occurs. Apoptotic death is highly regulated and energy dependent. It occurs in response to certain cellular signals or in the absence of others. There are at least three signaling pathways that trigger apoptosis by using caspase enzymes: the extrinsic (death receptor) pathway, the intrinsic (mitochondrial) pathway, and the perforin/granzyme pathway. The pathways are related, and all three converge on the same terminal or execution pathway.[22] (Clever cell biologists named some members of these pathways to recognize the proteins' participation in death signaling. RIP and KILLER participate

---

21. A. Saraste and K. Pulkki, "Morphologic and Biochemical Hallmarks of Apoptosis," *Cardiovascular Research* 45, no. 3 (February 2000): 528–37.
22. Susan Elmore, "Apoptosis: A Review of Programmed Cell Death," *Toxicologic Pathology* 35, no. 4 (2007): 495–516, https://doi.org/10.1080/01926230701320337.

in the extrinsic pathway and DIABLO in the intrinsic pathway, for example.)

Scientists believe that apoptosis is as important for the proper development and function of organisms as cell division is. Organisms are full of examples. The nervous system develops by first overproducing cells. Those cells that fail to establish functional synaptic connections die by apoptosis.[23] Apoptosis generates the space in our temporal bone for the middle ear and separates our fingers and toes so they are not webbed, as they are early in development.[24] My favorite example of the role apoptosis plays in the normal function of vertebrates is the immune system. Apoptosis is the default fate of many cells of the immune system. Both B and T lymphocytes undergo developmental processes that includes apoptosis. B lymphocytes are a kind of white blood cell (leukocyte). Their primary function is to produce antibodies, proteins that recognize foreign substances (viruses, bacteria, pollen, etc.) with great specificity and mark them for removal or destruction. The total number of different antibodies our B lymphocytes can produce is called our antibody repertoire. Immunologists estimate that our antibody repertoire is between one hundred million and ten trillion different antibodies.[25] Our genome is not large enough to encode one hundred million antibody genes. Instead of many genes, B lymphocytes

---

23. Deepak Nijhawan, Narimon Honarpour, and Xiaodong Wang, "Apoptosis in Neural Development and Disease," *Annual Review of Neuroscience* 23 (2000): 73–87, https://doi.org/10.1146/annurev.neuro.23.1.73.
24. John W. Saunders Jr., "Death in Embryonic Systems," *Science* 154, no. 3749 (November 4, 1966): 604, https://doi.org/10.1126/science.154.3749.604; Neal Anthwal and Hannah Thompson, "The Development of the Mammalian Outer and Middle Ear," *Journal of Anatomy* 228, no. 2 (February 2016): 217–32, https://doi.org/10.1111/joa.12344.
25. Roger R Beerli and Christoph Rader, "Mining Human Antibody Repertoires," *MAbs* 2, no. 4 (2010): 365–78, https://doi.org/10.4161/mabs.2.4.12187.

create this amazingly large repertoire using two random processes: somatic recombination and the insertion of nucleotides at the junctions between recombined segments of DNA. To produce part of an antibody, a heavy chain, B lymphocytes assemble a gene from three segments: one of many V segments is placed adjacent to one of several D segments and then adjacent to one of several J segments (V-D-J). Different combinations of Vs, Ds, and Js produce the diversity necessary for the antibody repertoire (V1-D2-J4 vs. V10-D1-J2 for example). To increase the number of different antibodies, B cells add uncoded nucleotides between the segments. The other part of an antibody, a light chain, is produced in a similar fashion. At the end of this process, each B lymphocyte has assembled a unique heavy chain gene and a unique light chain gene. Each B lymphocyte transcribes and translates a different antibody protein from these assembled genes. The antibody proteins constructed at the end of somatic recombination may not encounter a pathogen (virus, bacterium, or parasite) in the lifetime of the host. However, just in case it does, the immune system is ready to respond. The random process of generating the large antibody repertoire that we need makes us ready to react against pathogens that may not even be present on our planet yet. HIV-1 probably originated from SIV in the 1940s or 1950s, and Zika emerged as a human pathogen in the 1940s. Even before they were a threat, people already had B lymphocytes that were prepared to synthesize antibodies specific for these emerging pathogens. This is great news for us (and other species) who do not want to become extinct due to emerging infectious diseases.

The random process also generates many nonproductive rearrangements. Sometimes the nucleotides that are randomly inserted between segments create a premature stop codon. A protein produced by such a gene would be truncated and nonfunctional. If somatic recombination results in a nonproductive rearrangement, the cell has a few opportunities to try to re-rearrange its gene segments. Hopefully, the new gene rearrangement encodes a productive antibody protein, but if a cell runs out of possible attempts at rearranging and still has not produced a combination of gene segments that produces a functional antibody protein, the cell undergoes apoptosis. There is no need to keep a cell around if it cannot do what it needs to do to contribute to the well-being of the organism. Producing such an antibody is a waste of an organism's resources. In addition to nonproductive rearrangements, some of the productive rearrangements result in genes that encode an antibody that binds to self-proteins. Allowed to persist in the body, these autoreactive antibodies can lead to tissue destruction and autoimmune diseases. To prevent cells that produce autoreactive antibodies from causing problems, cells in the bone marrow test the antibodies that B lymphocytes produce. Immunologists call this process negative selection. If a B lymphocyte produces an antibody that is autoreactive, it fails to get the necessary survival signal and the cell dies by apoptosis. For B lymphocytes, programmed cell death is the default pathway. Survival requires a special signal. Scientists estimate that approximately 50 percent of B lymphocytes do not accomplish a productive, non-self-reactive rearrangement, and thus fail to make an antibody protein that might be useful to the host. These cells die by apoptosis.

T lymphocytes undergo a similar process in the thymus, a lymphatic organ near the heart. Somatic recombination and the insertion of random nucleotides at segment junctions produces two genes, alpha and beta, that together make up T cell receptors (TCR). Nonproductive rearrangements occur as they do when B lymphocytes form genes for antibodies. Like B lymphocytes, T lymphocytes get to make more than one attempt at rescuing a nonproductive TCR gene. Like B lymphocytes, many T lymphocytes fail to produce a TCR, and their fate is apoptosis. TCRs bind antigen differently than antibodies do. T lymphocytes must have antigens presented to them by an MHC protein much like a waiter presents an artfully arranged entrée to the guest at their restaurant. The TCR does not bind only the antigen but also binds the MHC molecule that presents the antigen. TCRs are, thus, MHC restricted. They must be able to bind the MHC proteins we express. MHC genes are among the most highly polymorphic of all genes. This means that the precise combination of MHC proteins any one individual expresses is most likely different from the combination of MHC proteins another individual expresses. The process of limiting T lymphocytes to those that assemble TCRs that are MHC restricted is called positive selection. More than 95 percent of all cells on their way to becoming T lymphocytes fail positive selection, and they die by apoptosis. The few cells that are MHC restricted and receive survival signals are tested for autoreactivity much like antibodies are. Only if cells are MHC restricted and do not bind self antigens do they receive the survival signals they need to complete the process of maturation and become mature T lymphocytes. This rigorous selection process, which most cells fail, ensures that the immune system is efficient and effective.

A functional immune system uses random processes, somatic recombination, and nucleotide addition in conjunction with selection to construct the B and T lymphocyte repertoire each vertebrate organism needs to fight the pathogens it will encounter over a lifetime. Death is built into this process to ensure that all lymphocytes produce

TCRs that are MHC restricted and no TCRs or antibodies are autoreactive. Without apoptosis, we would not survive our own immune systems. Out of cellular death comes an organismal life that flourishes.

Autophagy and Suffering

Cells employ many different methods of eliminating worn out proteins and organelles. Cells also need to break down proteins that ribosomes made incorrectly or were misfolded in the endoplasmic reticulum. Some signaling pathways degrade proteins that are part of the pathway as a way to prolong a signal. The signaling pathway that results in the translocation of NF-κB from the cytosol to the nucleus where it turns on the expression of specific genes uses protein degradation. Unstimulated cells that use the NF-κB pathway retain NF-κB in the cytosol, away from the DNA it could regulate, by keeping it bound to an inhibitor protein, I-κB. When the cells receive a signal, a cascade of intracellular events occurs, like tipping the first in a series of dominos. Near the end of the series of falling dominos, an enzyme modifies I-κB. Modified I-κB is a target of another enzyme that adds a string of ubiquitin units to I-κB. This ubiquitin tag is a signal to send the tagged protein to a proteasome. The proteasome is a large barrel-shaped protein complex. Proteins are fed into the barrel and exit as small, degraded fragments. When the proteasome degrades I-κB, NF-κB is free to move from the cytoplasm to the nucleus and change gene expression. The signal persists because in order to turn it off, the cell must synthesize more I-κB.

Lysosomes also participate in eliminating worn out proteins and organelles. Lysosomes are membrane-bound organelles filled with acid hydrolases. They are present in most eukaryotic cells. Christian de Duve discovered lysosomes in the 1950s and received the Nobel Prize for his work in 1974.[26] Acid hydrolases are enzymes that function best at a pH that is slightly lower than the pH of the cytosol. Acid pumps in the lysosomal membranes establish and maintain the pH difference. Acid hydrolases degrade many types of macromolecules, including proteins, nucleic acids, lipids, and carbohydrates. That they function optimally at low pH protects cells. If a lysosome ruptures and spills these degradative enzymes into the cytosol, the cytosol's neutral pH quickly inactivates them so they cannot degrade useful biomolecules in the cytosol. Worn out organelles or membrane-bound compartments that form as a result of phagocytosis (cell eating) can fuse with lysosomes. The fusion forms an autophagolysosome and delivers lysosomal degradative enzymes to more complex structures, such as whole organelles, for degradation.

Until the 1990s, scientists believed that autophagolysosomes were responsible only for the routine turnover of cellular proteins and organelles. They degraded proteins and organelles whose roles were finished and recycled their unit molecules and other components for use in building new cellular biomolecules. Yoshinori Ohsumi's laboratory studied the equivalent of autophagolysosomes in baker's yeast, *Saccharomyces cerevisiae*. *S. cerevisiae* is a simple eukaryotic system that allowed Ohsumi to study genetic mutants that were defective in degradative pathways or to study the degradative pathways in the presence of drugs that blocked protease activity.[27]

When Ohsumi's laboratory group placed yeast that

---

26. "Christian de Duve: Facts," The Nobel Prize, https://tinyurl.com/y7tge54x.
27. K. Takeshige, M. Baba, S. Tsuboi, T. Noda, and Y. Ohsumi, "Autophagy in Yeast Demonstrated with Proteinase-Deficient Mutants and Conditions for

carried a defective protease into nutrient-deficient media, they observed that vacuoles (the equivalent of autophagolysosomes in other eukaryotic cells) containing spherical structures accumulated after only one hour. After three hours, the vacuoles were almost completely full of spherical structures. They examined the contents of the vacuoles using electron microscopy and found that the spherical structures appeared to be miniature membrane-bound packets of cytosol, complete with cytoplasmic structures—endoplasmic reticulum, ribosomes, mitochondria, and more. Recognizing the similarity to autophagolysosomes, Ohsumi and colleagues called these membrane-bound structures autophagic bodies.[28] While cell biologists had described autophagolysosomes for decades, the conditions that induced their formation and the molecular mechanisms of autophagy were still unknown. Ohsumi's work provided an important clue. These autophagic bodies accumulated if the cells were unable to degrade proteins because they carried a gene that encoded a nonfunctional protease or if they were treated with protease inhibitor. If cells were grown in media depleted of nitrogen, carbon, sulfate, phosphate, or single essential amino acids, or if the cells were placed under other stress-inducing conditions, autophagic bodies formed.[29] Ohsumi's laboratory quickly began to dissect the process of autophagy—the destruction of damaged or redundant cellular components in cellular vacuoles. They reported discovering and characterizing

Its Induction," *The Journal of Cell Biology* 119, no. 2 (October 1992): 301–11.

28. Takeshige et al., "Autophagy in Yeast," 301–11.
29. Takeshige et al., "Autophagy in Yeast," 301–11; Ian G. Ganley, Pui-Mon Wong, Noor Gammoh, Xuejun Jiang, "Distinct Autophagosomal-Lysosomal Fusion Mechanism Revealed by Thapsigargin-Induced Autophagy Arrest," *Molecular Cell* 42, no. 6 (June 24, 2011): 731–43, https://doi.org/10.1016/j.molcel.2011.04.024.

fourteen new *ATG* (AuTophaGy-related) genes in 1998.[30] This novel method for ridding cells of worn-out proteins and organelles used a system that resembled the ubiquitin-ligase system we saw in NF-κB regulation. In the ATG system, Apg7/Atg7 links a glycine amino acid at the carboxy-end of Apg12/Atg12 (a small, 186–amino acid protein) to a lysine amino acid of a slightly larger (294–amino acid) protein, Apg5/Atg5. The Atg12/Atg5 complex binds Atg16 and together these proteins promote the formation of an autophagosome by expanding a small membrane cisternae (isolation membrane) so that it surrounds a portion of the cytosol.[31] The isolation membrane eventually seals to form a double-membrane vacuole called the autophagosome. The auto-phagosome fuses with a lysosome, and its contents are degraded by acid hydrolases. During his impressive career, Ohsumi and his colleagues identified forty-one yeast *ATG* genes and, not surprisingly given the predictions of evolutionary theory, most of these have orthologues in higher eukaryotes, including humans.[32] In 2016, Yoshinori Ohsumi was awarded the Nobel Prize in Physiology or Medicine for his groundbreaking work.

Scientists in a wide variety of fields now study autophagy and have found that it is essential to normal

---

30. N. Mizushima et al., "A Protein Conjugation System Essential for Autophagy," *Nature* 395, no. 6700 (September 24, 1998): 395–98, https://doi.org/10.1038/26506.
31. Jong Ok Pyo, Jihoon Nah, and Yong-Keun Jung, "Molecules and Their Functions in Autophagy," *Experimental & Molecular Medicine* 44, no. 2 (2012): 73–80, https://doi.org/10.3858/emm.2012.44.2.029.
32. Margaret M. Harnett, Miguel A. Pineda, Perle Latré de Laté, Russell J. Eason, Sébastien Besteiro, William Harnett, and Gordon Langsley, "From Christian de Duve to Yoshinori Ohsumi: More to Autophagy Than Just Dining at Home," *Biomedical Journal* 40, no. 1 (February 2017): 9–22, https://doi.org/10.1016/j.bj.2016.12.004.

cellular development and differentiation.[33] Autophagy dysregulation is implicated in the etiology of cancer, obesity, aging, diabetes, and neurodegenerative disorders such as Alzheimer's disease, Parkinson's disease, and Huntington's chorea.[34] It is also clear that autophagy occurs not only in isolated cells like yeast but in multicellular animals as well. De Duve and colleagues induced autophagy in the livers of rats when they treated rats with glucagon, a hormone that opposes the action of insulin and is secreted

33. Francesca Vittoria Sbrana, Margherita Cortini, Sofia Avnet, Francesca Perut, Marta Columbaro, Angelo De Milito, and Nicola Baldini, "The Role of Autophagy in the Maintenance of Stemness and Differentiation of Mesenchymal Stem Cells," *Stem Cell Reviews* 12, no. 6 (2016): 621–33, https://doi.org/10.1007/s12015-016-9690-4; Meng Li, Ping Gao, and Junping Zhang, "Crosstalk between Autophagy and Apoptosis: Potential and Emerging Therapeutic Targets for Cardiac Diseases," *International Journal of Molecular Sciences* 17, no. 3 (March 2016): 332, https://doi.org/10.3390/ijms17030332; Mizushima et al., "Protein Conjugation System," 395–98; Jisun Lee, Samantha Giordano, and Jianhua Zhang, "Autophagy, Mitochondria and Oxidative Stress: Cross-Talk and Redox Signalling," *Biochemical Journal* 441, no. 2 (January 15, 2012): 523–40, https://doi.org/10.1042/BJ20111451.
34. Álvaro F. Fernández et al., "Autophagy Couteracts Weight Gain, Lipotoxicity and Pancreatic β-Cell Death upon Hypercaloric pro-Diabetic Regimens," *Cell Death & Disease* 8, no. 8 (August 3, 2017): e2970, https://doi.org/10.1038/cddis.2017.373; Sayaka Inokuchi-Shimizu et al., "TAK1-Mediated Autophagy and Fatty Acid Oxidation Prevent Hepatosteatosis and Tumorigenesis," *The Journal of Clinical Investigation* 124, no. 8 (July 1, 2014): 3566–78, https://doi.org/10.1172/JCI74068; Congcong He et al., "Exercise-Induced BCL2-Regulated Autophagy Is Required for Muscle Glucose Homeostasis," *Nature* 481, no. 7382 (January 18, 2012): 511–15, https://doi.org/10.1038/nature10758; Ju Huang and Daniel J. Klionsky, "Autophagy and Human Disease," *Cell Cycle* 6, no. 15 (August 1, 2007): 1837–49, https://doi.org/10.4161/cc.6.15.4511; Pyo, Nah, and Jung, "Molecules and Their Functions"; Ichiro Nakagawa et al., "Autophagy Defends Cells against Invading Group A Streptococcus," *Science* 306, no. 5698 (November 5, 2004): 1037–40, https://doi.org/10.1126/science.1103966.

under low blood sugar conditions.[35] Another research group treated rats with insulin, a hormone that opposes the action of glucagon, and documented an inhibition of autophagy in cells of the kidney.[36] Additional studies observed autophagy induction in the urinary bladder, skeletal and cardiac muscle, and most other tissue types where scientists have looked for it, including the lens of the eye, pancreas, muscle, and thymus.[37]

Scientists now recognize that autophagy is a complex, highly regulated, highly conserved, essential response to conditions of starvation.[38] Autophagy seems to be a ubiquitous process that is essential for eukaryotic cells and organisms.[39] Yeast carrying defective or nonfunctional variants of genes involved in autophagy (*ATG* genes) quickly die

35. R. L. Deter and C. De Duve, "Influence of Glucagon, an Inducer of Cellular Autophagy, on Some Physical Properties of Rat Liver Lysosomes," *Journal of Cell Biology* 33, no. 2 (May 1967): 437–49.
36. U. Pfeifer and M. Warmuth-Metz, "Inhibition by Insulin of Cellular Autophagy in Proximal Tubular Cells of Rat Kidney," *American Journal of Physiology* 244, no. 2 (February 1983): E109–114, https://doi.org/10.1152/ajpendo.1983.244.2.E109.
37. Andreja Erman, Nataša Resnik, and Rok Romih, "Autophagic Activity in the Mouse Urinary Bladder Urothelium as a Response to Starvation," *Protoplasma* 250, no. 1 (February 2013): 151–60, https://doi.org/10.1007/s00709-012-0387-5; He et al., "Exercise-Induced BCL2-Regulated Autophagy," 511–15; Noboru Mizushima, Akitsugu Yamamoto, Makoto Matsui, Tamotsu Yoshimori, and Yoshinori Ohsumi, "In Vivo Analysis of Autophagy in Response to Nutrient Starvation Using Transgenic Mice Expressing a Fluorescent Autophagosome Marker," *Molecular Biology of the Cell* 15, no. 3 (March 2004): 1101–11, https://doi.org/10.1091/mbc.E03-09-0704.
38. Mizushima et al., "Protein Conjugation," 395–98; Yoshinori Ohsumi, "Historical Landmarks of Autophagy Research," *Cell Research* 24, no. 1 (January 2014): 9–23, https://doi.org/10.1038/cr.2013.169.
39. Alicia Meléndez and Thomas P. Neufeld, "The Cell Biology of Autophagy in Metazoans: A Developing Story," *Development* 135, no. 14 (August 2008): 2347–60, https://doi.org/10.1242/dev.016105.

when placed in starvation conditions.[40] *Drosophila melanogaster* (fruit flies) and *Caenorhabditis elegans* (tiny soil-dwelling worms) require properly functioning *ATG* genes for development.[41] Even plants need *ATG* genes. When *Arabidopsis thaliana* (a small plant in the mustard family often used for genetic studies) carries variants of *ATG* genes that are defective, they age at a higher rate than plants with properly functioning *ATG* genes.[42] Indeed, it appears that autophagy prevents or delays the cellular and organismal events we associate with aging.

Finding that a form of self-cannibalism is critical for cellular and organismal well-being was surprising to scientists. They wondered what kinds of possible benefits autophagy could provide to cells and whole organisms and how those benefits might lead to a reduction in disease incidence, increased health, and longer lifespans. Cells were destroying their own protein and organelles: the very proteins and organelles the cell expended enormous

---

40. Miki Tsukada and Yoshinori Ohsumi, "Isolation and Characterization of Autophagy-Defective Mutants of Saccharomyces Cerevisiae," *FEBS Letters* 333, no. 1–2 (October 25, 1993): 169–74.
41. Hai Wu, Meng C. Wang, and Dirk Bohmann, "JNK Protects *Drosophila* from Oxidative Stress by Trancriptionally Activating Autophagy," *Mechanisms of Development* 126, no. 8–9 (2009): 624–37, https://doi.org/10.1016/j.mod.2009.06.1082; Meléndez and Neufeld, "Cell Biology of Autophagy," 2347–60.
42. Jed H. Doelling, Joseph M. Walker, Eric M. Friedman, Allison R. Thompson, and Richard D. Vierstra, "The APG8/12-Activating Enzyme APG7 Is Required for Proper Nutrient Recycling and Senescence in *Arabidopsis thaliana*," *Journal of Biological Chemistry* 277, no. 36 (September 6, 2002): 33,105–14, https://doi.org/10.1074/jbc.M204630200; Hideki Hanaoka, Takeshi Noda, Yumiko Shirano, Tomohiko Kato, Hiroaki Hayashi, Daisuke Shibata, Satoshi Tabata, Yoshinori Ohsumi, "Leaf Senescence and Starvation-Induced Chlorosis Are Accelerated by the Disruption of an Arabidopsis Autophagy Gene," *Plant Physiology* 129, no. 3 (July 2002): 1181–93, https://doi.org/10.1104/pp.011024.

amounts of energy to build. Moreover, cells were tearing down these valuable commodities under conditions that seemed to demand that each organelle and each protein work its hardest: starvation.

Maybe scientists should not have been so surprised. Ecologists had been observing life-death balance in thriving ecosystems for decades. We know that the pain we suffer when we push ourselves in the gym has a pay-off in the end. My students endure hours of studying, sacrificing their social life, so they can earn a good grade in my course and eventually acceptance into graduate school. Any of us who have been in an intimate relationship or friendship know that denying our own desires is sometimes necessary to nurture that relationship. Every autumn Sunday afternoon, I go to the family room rather than putter in my garden to watch the Kansas City Chiefs play because it is important to my husband and therefore to our marriage.

Maybe scientists who are Christians should have recognized something essential to their Christian faith echoing in the lessons of autophagy since, every Sunday, together we point to the cross as the supreme demonstration of love as sacrifice, death, and suffering. In Romans 5, Paul tells us to "boast in our sufferings, knowing that suffering produces endurance, and endurance produces character, and character produces hope, and hope does not disappoint us, because God's love has been poured into our hearts through the Holy Spirit that has been given to us" (Ro 5:3–5). Maybe self-cannibalism is not the best description of what the cells were doing. Maybe a better image is the refiner's fire of Zechariah 13:9 or the pruning of John 15:2: "He removes every branch in me that bears no fruit. Every branch that bears fruit he prunes to make it bear more fruit." Sacrifice and destruction make room for us to build something that can flourish. These images make sense in light of autophagy, apoptosis, and ecological systems because, although each of these processes includes destruction, none of the processes are recklessly or indiscriminately destructive.

Predators preferentially prey on weaker animals. In doing so, they strengthen the whole prey population. Apoptosis and autophagy are tightly regulated and intentional processes. Autophagy selects old, misfolded, worn out, broken, dead proteins and cells for degradation in autophagolysosomes, mirroring the culling that wolves do to the moose population. Cells are similarly culling their organelles and proteins, using the amino acids from misfolded proteins to build new ones. Nutrients bound up in cells that died by apoptosis or in excess organelles are released upon degradation so they can be redirected for use in processes that are more critical for cell flourishing. Cardiac muscle cells depend on mitochondria to produce the energy they need to maintain their rhythmic contraction throughout our lifetime. Old mitochondria slow down. Autophagy breaks down slow mitochondria so cardiac muscle cells can replace them with new, healthy ones. Proteins in our neurons become damaged, and others fold improperly. Over time, these proteins form tangled networks that can damage the cells critical for sending the signals that allow us to think, create, remember, learn, and much more. Autophagy helps to identify these dangerous proteins and remove them.

The universal trigger for autophagy seems to be nutrient deprivation. Starvation. Cells deprived of nitrogen or carbon find the elements they cannot get from their environment in the worn out bits of themselves. In times of plenty, these worn out bits are ignored, but when cells cannot get what they need from their environment, the cells become essentialists. They break down everything that is not necessary for survival and use the building blocks to remake what they need to persist through these times of stress.

There is a growing body of scientific evidence that short periods of starvation are not only good for cells but also for organisms. Organisms, including humans, that undergo short, repeated periods of fasting are healthier and live longer.[43] Restricting calorie intake induces autophagy, resulting in healthier cells and healthier bodies. Autophagy mediates the protection of essential organ functions including the liver, heart, kidney, and nervous system. Can we glean a truth that is consistent with scriptural truth from an understanding of suffering, sacrifice, and death in light of evolutionary theory and the natural world? Jesus himself used a biological image to teach about his impending death, saying, "Unless a grain of wheat falls into the earth and dies, it remains just a single grain; but if it dies, it bears much fruit" (John 12:24). Sacrifice, suffering, and death seem built into the natural world—necessary for its flourishing. Sacrifice, death, and suffering are as essential to life as reproduction, biosynthesis, and metabolism. Christians see this truth in the life we receive through the death and resurrection of Christ. The gospels portray death as the ultimate expression of love in Christ's sacrifice and the door through which God chose to usher in God's new kingdom. Restoration and flourishing from suffering and death. It is true for our cells. It is true for our bodies. It is true for our embodied souls. It is a truth of our faith. Just as the death of an organism allows for the rebirth and flourishing

---

43. David C. Rubinsztein, Guillermo Mariño, and Guido Kroemer, "Autophagy and Aging," *Cell* 146, no. 5 (September 2, 2011): 682–95, https://doi.org/10.1016/j.cell.2011.07.030; Frank Madeo, Andreas Zimmermann, Maria Chiara Maiuri, and Guido Kroemer, "Essential Role for Autophagy in Life Span Extension," *Journal of Clinical Investigation* 125, no. 1 (January 2015): 85–93, https://doi.org/10.1172/JCI73946.

of life, so the death of Jesus leads to a rebirth and new life for Jesus's followers. "Degradation is a fundamental cellular function, just as essential to the functioning of life as synthesis."[44] Biologists see that processes that appear to be destructive—apoptosis, autophagy, evolution, and ecological systems—are essential to a flourishing life. Perhaps the essentiality of destructive processes hints at the way God acts to redeem death for the sake of new and flourishing life.

---

44. Ohsumi, "Historical Landmarks of Autophagy Research," 20.

8.

Embracing Our Animal: Youth Ministry in a Secular₃ World

Jason Lief

> Christianity is less a religion of formal ritual and worship than a return to human personhood.
> —Ilia Delio, *The Unbearable Wholeness of Being*

Luke's Gospel tells the story of two disappointed and cynical disciples traveling from Jerusalem to Emmaus. They thought Jesus was the messiah—the one who would restore Israel to her rightful place. Instead, he was crucified by the Romans—a tragic end to their messianic hopes and dreams. As they make their way along the road, a stranger begins walking with them. He asks what they're talking about, to which they respond: "Are you the only stranger in Jerusalem who does not know the things that have taken place there in these days?" (Luke 24:18) "What things?" (Luke 24:19) comes the reply. And so they explain what happened. He tells them how thickheaded they've been ("Oh, how foolish you are, and how slow of heart to believe all that the prophets have declared" [Luke 24:25]), as he interprets the Old Testament story. When it looks like the stranger is going to continue on, they invite him in. Luke tells it this way: "When he was at the table with them, he took bread, blessed and broke it, and gave it to them. Then their eyes were opened, and the recognized him; and he vanished from their sight" (Luke 24:30–31). To their astonishment, the stranger on the road was Jesus.

What was it that kept these two disciples from recognizing him? Clearly, they expected something to happen on the third day—they alluded to the news that the tomb was empty. And yet, as Jesus walked with them on the road, they did not recognize him. So, why did they recognize him when he broke the bread? What was it about that particular act that caused their eyes to be opened? In his essay "They Recognized Him; and He Became Invisible to Them," Jean Luc Marion suggests their lack of imagination is to blame, saying, "They do not recognize him because they cannot even imagine that this is really him who has rejoined them, so far do their poor, cobbled-together, honest-to-goodness concepts find themselves outstripped by 'events' that leave them petrified within a matrix of irrefutable prejudices."[1] Put differently, their way of thinking about the world, their way of imagining the world, was lacking. They were incapable of recognizing the resurrected Christ because he didn't fit into their conceptual framework—resurrection didn't fit how they thought the world worked. Jesus was dead, and they lacked the imagination to see it any other way.

Marion refers to the breaking of the bread in this story as a "saturated phenomenon." This is when events overwhelm our concepts, our language, our framework—everything we use to make sense of the world. Marion argues these are experiences that show reality to be much deeper and more complex than we imagine. This is the experience of the disciples when Jesus breaks the bread. It draws them back to the final supper Jesus had with his followers, allowing the two disciples to finally see who the stranger is—the resur-

---

1. Jean-Luc Marion, "They Recognized Him; and He Became Invisible to Them," *Modern Theology* 18, no. 2 (December 2002): 147.

rected Christ. The bread and the act of eating, something we think we know, in this moment becomes the uncontainable revelation of the resurrected Christ.

So, what does this have to do with evolution and youth ministry? Too often, our response to new theological and scientific insights is a lack of imagination because our conceptual and theological framework is too frail and thin. We think we see straight; we think we have God all figured out. So we see opposition to evolution as some kind of heroic act to defend the Christian faith. However, as the Pew Research shows, that young people increasingly don't buy it—opting out of organized religion for less archaic views of reality. Unfortunately, the response of many in the Christian community is to see this as some form of martyrdom, so they double down on hyperliteral approaches to the Bible and hyperspiritual forms of piety that reduce truth to objective facts, making sure our experience of God and our understanding of the world matches our conceptual framework.

Compounding the problem is the inability of the church to provide young people with a Christian story that can sustain reality. The well-known work of Christian Smith, Kenda Dean, Chap Clark, and Andrew Root speaks about the consequences of giving our young people a Christian story that is too thin. As I speak to youth pastors, church leaders, and young people, I hear them talk about the importance of relationships and the power of stories; what they don't talk about, however, is the depth of relationships and the complexity of language that constructs our identity. Focusing on relationships and experiences without providing a robust way to make sense of the world means we're not providing young people with the tools they need to address their lived experience. Reducing reality and the Bible to provable facts drains the mystery from everything, forcing young people to turn to other cultural stories to find meaning. Increasingly, young people struggle to make sense of their embodied life in this world because the adult world hasn't given them much to work with. The complexity of their questions, their struggles, and their experiences of the world are met with a thin version of the Christian story that is not able to hold up under the weight of their questions. What are their questions, and how might a Christian dialogue with evolution point the way to a more robust theological story? That's what this chapter is about.

Secular$_2$ in a Secular$_3$ World

In his book *Faith Formation in a Secular Age*, Andrew Root discusses the deeper philosophical and cultural issues facing the contemporary church.[2] He uses Charles Taylor's *A Secular Age* to explore the influence of secularity on contemporary Western culture. Following Taylor, he describes three forms of the secular that have developed in the West over the past five hundred years. The first (secular$_1$) interprets the sacred and secular realms as two distinct planes, one higher (sacred) and the other lower (secular). The result is a hierarchal view of reality, with the sacred above the secular. Both spheres are good, but they are different. An example of this from the Middle Ages is the way the monastic life was seen as a "higher calling" than the ordinary life of, say, a farmer or blacksmith. Both were considered good, but one was seen as more spiritual, or higher, than the other. Another example is how the institutional church, with the priest or pastor as leader, mediated the sacred to the world through beliefs and practices. The

---

2. Andrew Root, *Faith Formation in a Secular Age: Responding to the Church's Obsession with Youthfulness* (Grand Rapids: Baker, 2017).

liturgical year was seen as a higher form of time, sacred time, that people and communities participated in as part of the life of the church. I remember as a high-school student attending a Catholic school, we were required to attend morning mass whenever we had a basketball or football game. If we didn't go to mass, we didn't play. Why? The ordinary activity of basketball or football needed to be caught up into the sacred through the priest and the Eucharist. We didn't win every game, but going to Mass was a way to bring these activities into the realm of the sacred.

The second version (secular$_2$) is associated with the Reformation—the sacred and secular are no longer seen on different planes but reinterpreted as different spaces. There is secular space (football, basketball, plumbing, and ballet), and there is sacred space, which is the space of the spiritual within the institutional church. These spaces are not higher or lower; the spiritual and the cultural spheres are on the same level. This means being a plumber is not a lesser calling; it is a calling of a different kind. One way to make sense of this is to use the two-kingdoms approach to the relationship between the secular and the sacred. We don't go to a pastor or priest to figure out how to fix our car, we go to a mechanic. The work of a mechanic is a vocation, a calling from God, that is a valuable part of culture, and Christians are to serve God throughout these vocations that are part of the secular sphere. To experience God's grace and salvation, however, one must go to the sacred space of the church where the preaching of the word and the sacraments (the means of grace) are found. The label *two kingdoms* is misleading because both are good, and people are to live in both. However, salvation is only found in the sacred space, through the preaching of the word and the sacraments, within the institutional church. Because of this, the emphasis of the church in secular$_2$ is institutional affiliation. Within secular space, this means being connected to the social institutions of family, government, vocation, and so on. Within the sacred space, however, it means being connected with the church. Root describes how this view of the sacred and secular means that the purpose of youth ministry is to keep young people connected to the church. When they leave the church, they leave the sacred and abandon faith.

The final version, secular$_3$, is the absence of transcendence, which means it is the absence of any sacred/secular divide. This is the current cultural experience of the West, where there is no sacred space, which means institutions like the church lose their significance. In its place is a new form of spirituality deeply connected to experience, where spirituality is just as likely, if not more likely, to be found at a rock concert or craft beer pub as the church.

This is why people immersed within secular$_3$ are more likely to put their trust in science, technology, economics, or politics as the sources of immanent power that brings change and transformation. Some may hold on to church, but it merely exists as one experience among many. This is where Root makes an important observation about the problem confronting youth ministry. He writes,

> The reason faith formation is so difficult is that we have failed to see how our imagination is caught in the rut of secular$_2$. In this rut we've erroneously interpreted our issues through secular$_2$, believing that the real issue of faith formation is the loss, or revealed impotence, of the (institutional) church. . . . Nearly all of today's most popular faith-formation perspectives are driven by imaginary of secular$_2$. . . . We add adjectives to "faith" because in the end faith is not about divine action but about maintaining religious space. We need faith that is robust, vital, and sticky so young people con-

tinue to believe, and participate, in such a way that the space of the religious is maintained.[3]

Viewing faith as affiliation means that for young people to be saved, they need to be connected to the church. This means the task of youth ministry is to connect young people to the church by either keeping them connected or getting them reconnected. It does this by providing experiences and relationships. Root's work doesn't call into question the importance of institutions; he does, however, suggest that this is not how young people experience spirituality. Immersed within the secular$_3$ paradigm, they do not see institutions as either sacred or secular. They want spirituality, but they don't care about the institutional church. They want to experience or encounter God, but they don't care about denominational loyalty. In other words, Root insightfully suggests that contemporary youth ministry often addresses the issue of faith formation from an outdated perspective—trying to keep young people connected to institutions they don't care about.

The negative side of secular$_3$ is that the institutional church has lost influence. This has caused many churches to become obsessed with new programs, constantly reinventing themselves to attract young people and emergent adults. Not that reinvention is always bad, but with the increasing speed of fads and technology, it's an endless cycle of anxiety and reinvention. The positive side of secular$_3$ is that young people and emergent adults take their lived experience in this world much more seriously. Young people are passionate about issues of justice and the environment, and they are passionate about organic food and new ways of living. The problem with youth ministry as it often exists is that it fails to match the depth of this

---

3. Root, *Faith Formation*, 108.

new reality. The unquenchable search for spirituality and experience, as well as the questions and issues they face, are often met with a thin version of Christianity that is unable to sustain their lived experience. When it comes to issues of sexuality, justice, economics, or the environment, youth ministry has not provided the biblical or theological tools to help young people cultivate an imagination to make sense of the world. Here, the moralistic and dogmatic answers that are provided foster new forms of anxiety and fear as their experience of life does not match up to the unrealistic and unhealthy expectations. This is where the rubber hits the road regarding evolution and youth ministry.

Secular$_3$ assumes a scientific worldview that takes the experiences of this world seriously. It is open to conversations about science, economics, and politics. These conversations lead to important questions pertaining to human identity and the meaning of human experience. So much so that sometimes the language used to describe these experiences is language once used for religious belief. Whether it's the draw of extreme sports that bring people the exhilaration of limit experiences, the experience of different cultures, or an encounter with the natural world, these experiences often overwhelm our concepts and intuitions like the disciples on the road to Emmaus. These experiences point to a deeper form of spirituality that recognizes there is more to the material world than meets the eye. Like the disciples, people are awakened to transcendence not as some higher dimension but as a form of relational transcendence within the created world.

Our purpose has been to show how Christian faith is compatible with an evolutionary perspective. While this forces the Christian community to reorient the way we think about science and faith, it is an opportunity for us to help young people recognize how Christianity reveals the God who is present in their experience and encounter of the created world. It allows us the possibility of reframing how we think about God and the revelation of God in the incarnation of Jesus Christ. It helps us rethink what it means to be human in the context of Scripture, theology, and biology—recognizing how the lived experience of embodied life is affirmed by God in Jesus Christ. It moves the focus of faith away from institutions, away from abstract theological concepts, toward a true understanding of what we mean when we say that God is love.

Our purpose has been to show how the incarnation reveals that our human identity is grounded in our relationship with God and the created world. This leads to an immanent form of transcendence in which the revelation of God's love for the world in Jesus Christ opens up a way of knowing God and the world that is grounded in love. It is a way of love revealed in the death and resurrection of Jesus Christ that overcomes our tendency toward idolatry, the tendency to close ourselves off from God and the world by insisting on our own concepts, ideas, and ways of seeing the world. This is the problem with both a conservative and liberal theology. Both assume certain truths, whether they be theological or cultural, and impose them on God and the world. An incarnational theology insists that God comes to us, that God breaks us open, so we can encounter God in our neighbor and in the creation.

As Root makes clear, too often youth ministry engages young people while assuming $secular_2$—assuming that all we have to do is get young people to connect to a church and then they will encounter God. The thinking is that if we only keep them in the sacred space of an institution with practices that reinforce their participation, then we've done our job. The problem with this is that young people in the West increasingly do not believe in sacred space. They don't see the church or the school or political institutions as sacred. What evolution offers youth ministry and the Christian community is an opportunity to encounter transcendence within our embodied humanity as part of a larger web of life. Rather than trying to get young people to be Christian by adhering to abstract moral or doctrinal principles, or through praise and worship spectacles, a robust dialogue with evolution pushes young people back to the material creation, back to their bodies, back to their relationship with each other and the created world.

Embracing Our Animal

Elizabeth Johnson helps us see how Darwin was not trying to undermine religious experience—just the opposite. She writes,

> The young Charles found the natural world created by God beautiful and full of wonder; close observation of it brought him intense joy. As he reported at the Beagle's first stop at the Cape Verde Islands off the African coast to take on water: "The scene, as beheld through the hazy atmosphere of this climate, is one of great interest; if, indeed, a person, fresh from the sea, and who has just walked, for the first time, in a grove of cocoa-nut trees, can be the judge of anything but his own happiness." As he later recalled, this kind of personal experience of nature was intimately connected with a sense of God. Being outside in the natural world, interacting with it, filled his mind with feeling of "wonder, admiration, and devotion" directed to the One who created it, sublime beyond words.[4]

---

4. Elizabeth A. Johnson, *Ask the Beasts: Darwin and the God of Love* (London: Bloomsbury, 2014), 37.

Johnson admits that Darwin's religious beliefs changed as he went deeper into his theory of natural selection and survival of the fittest, but it is important to see how Darwin was driven by a love for the natural world, and a desire to look closely at material existence and the beauty, mystery, and wonder of a changing world. And this is exactly what young people need more of—looking closely. Everything about Western culture tries to get them to take their eyes off of the material. From Spotify to Snapchat, to sports and grades, the identity of young people is under the constant threat of abstraction. Increasingly, life is lived in the cloud, both literally and metaphorically. Darwin reminds us to look downward, to take seriously the stuff of this world and our place in it. Now, it's youth ministry's turn to take Darwin seriously, to take the Bible seriously, and to lay claim to the truth about Christianity—that in Jesus Christ God took on human flesh, entering into this embodied life, and by his mere presence, embraced it. So, what are the practical consequences of youth ministry taking the relationship between science and faith seriously? There are four primary areas in which this discussion will have a positive impact upon the lives of young people: how they view embodied life, how they view the created world, how they view spirituality, and how they view the church.

Embodied Life

Christianity has always struggled against various forms of Gnosticism that privileges a spiritualized version of human life over the body. It has its roots in a combined version of Greek philosophy and Christianity in the early centuries of the church, and it's never really gone away. Today, it takes the form of abstraction, where the true meaning of something is always found in the abstraction of the thing. The best example is money, which places a value on products and services (price) that often has nothing to do with the product itself. It's the reduction of lived experience to principles or numbers that point to some purified, perfect ideal held up as the "norm."

Take athletics. Increasingly, young people invest themselves in sports, spending time and money perfecting their skills, honing their form, trying to achieve more and more. Kids play organized sports at younger ages, often specializing in one sport in order to achieve success. And what is success? Winning? Always getting better? Improving? Championships? What's ironic about sports is that they should be places where embodiment is celebrated. After all, people use their bodies in sports; they shape and train their bodies, disciplining them to do what they want them to do. However, the language of sports brings these embodied activities under some higher cause—excellence, greatness, or, in Christian circles, bringing glory to God. How often is God invoked as the reason for winning a championship or making the winning shot? What's lost is the activity itself, playing, getting caught up in embodied activity that allows participants to lose awareness, to become connected with our instincts, or to be made aware of our limitations. What is also lost is the beauty of losing and the importance of failure. The constant pressure to achieve, or to succeed, is an unrealistic one. All failure is not sin, just as all imperfection is not sin. This is the message of evolution and of Christianity—it is more often glorious failure that leads to new creation. This is a message our young people desperately need to hear, and this is a place where science can contribute to youth ministry. A Christian engagement of sports cannot be focused on such abstractions; an evolutionary approach to athletics would embrace the material conditions that allow for chance, competition, and the beauty of embodied diversity.

Another important issue evolution and youth ministry can address together is sexuality. Too often the Christian community settles for purity propaganda on one side or cultural assimilation on the other. Both are unable to sustain the experiences of young people as they live into their sexuality. The purity emphasis ignores the embodied aspects of our humanity—that we are created beings with biological drives that develop and change. Holding to outdated and abstract notions of purity can have negative consequences as young people deny their sexuality, or it can lead to descriptive forms of shame if they do engage in various forms of sexual activity. On the flip side, just giving in to the cultural ideology of sexuality does not provide young people with a relational understanding of sex and the implications of promiscuity and pornography. As I tell my students, the problem with pornography is not the sex, it's that the sexual relationships are not real. Unfortunately, the Christian community struggles to find a middle ground between these two poles, usually falling on one side or the other.

An incarnational engagement of evolution provides a way to engage the issue of sexuality and gender biologically and biblically. Recognizing that humans are animals with sexual drives that are good and healthy allows youth ministry to present a positive, life-affirming view of sexuality. When the biology of sexuality is presented, young people are allowed to recognize the beauty and purpose of difference. We are not all created the same; we are all unique, embodied persons. We are able to recognize how the biological dimensions of sex and sexuality are important parts of what it means to be a human person made in the image of God. Not only does this affirm the goodness of sex and sexuality, but it also places them within in the context of transcendence and relationality. We approach God not as sexless spiritual beings but as sexual, embodied creatures. We encounter each other in the same way, which is why, biblically speaking, sex should occur within a covenantal commitment—what we call marriage. It has nothing to do with purity and everything to do with the vulnerability of sex as an act in which we are physically and spiritually laid bare before another person. Lew Smedes, in his book *Sex for Christians*, argues that because of this vulnerability and intimacy, sex is most life giving and life affirming within the context of committed vows and the promise to be faithful to each other.[5] Framing sex in this way provides young people with a positive reason why it should be reserved for marriage, while affirming it as a good part of our created being. In fact, Smedes recommends that physical intimacy needs to be part of a dating relationship, and that refraining from touching, holding hands, or kissing is unhealthy. Young people need to discover their sexuality in relationship with each other; they need to be given permission to explore each other's bodies within the boundaries of mutuality, respect, and love.

Closely related to this is helping young people recognize the goodness of diversity and difference. Increasingly, young people's lives are abstracted by technology and capitalism as they are institutionalized. Cultural messages of authenticity and creativity are a front for conformity. As young people see versions of the ideal life given to them by corporations and educational institutions, their lives are gripped by fear and anxiety as they fail to measure up. An engagement of evolutionary creationism creates space for difference and diversity, and it recognizes that the impulse

---

5. Lewis B. Smedes, *Sex for Christians: The Limits and Liberties of Sexual Living* (Grand Rapids: Eerdmans, 1994), 145.

of life is toward change and transformation. Embracing evolution and the theological categories that see creation as an expression of God's love allows young people to truly embrace their particularity—to embrace what makes them unique and irreplaceable as creatures made in the image of God.

Creation

An incarnational dialogue between evolution and faith reframes our relationship with the creation. Rather than seeing creation as an act that happened "in the beginning," evolution affirms the ongoing process of creation through the secondary causes embedded within the created world. This doesn't mean that God is somehow absent; it means that God's love created a world that is able to express new forms of life. In this way, all of creation can be interpreted as an expression of God's love, an expression of incarnation that culminates in the person of Jesus Christ. This means creation is not just an object or stage for the story of human redemption; it is a significant expression of the word spoken in the beginning as an expression of God's love. The creation is the expression of God's desire to dwell with creation that reaches its climax in the person of Jesus Christ.

This means that to be human is to be deeply connected with the creation; to live as human beings made in the image of God is to live as creatures and recognize that our lives are dependent upon our relationship to the created order. This interpretation of creation is important for young people living in the West. While there was a time when humanity struggled against nature to survive, technology has now led us to a moment in history where we are increasingly disconnected from the creation. As young people increasingly struggle with anxiety and depression, one response needs to be helping young people reconnect with creation. While youth ministry has always included camping and outdoor experiences, embracing an evolutionary perspective in conversation with theology opens us up to take "long looks" at the created world. It allows us to point young people to the ways in which our own form of life is bound up with the animals and the plants, the sky and the land. It provides an opportunity for the Christian community to frame our lives in relationship to the creation, that we are dependent upon it for life, and that the story of the relationship of God with God's people has always included the creation.

Barbara Brown Taylor speaks to this in her book *An Altar in the World*. She writes, "There is no substitute for earthiness. From dust we came and to dust we shall return. The good news is that most of us get some good years in between, during which we may sink our hands in the dirt. This is as good a way as any to recover our connection to the ground of all being. Digging down is as good a way to God as rising up, if only because you can feel it in your shoulders."[6] She goes on to talk about the hard work of taking care of the earth, of tending the garden. She writes, "You get dirty doing it. You break fingernails and wear holes in the knees of your pants. You wear yourself out."[7] But then she goes on to talk about how the act of immersing ourselves in the dirt reconnects us with a vital part of our humanity. She writes,

---

6. Barbara Brown Taylor, *An Altar in the World: Finding the Sacred beneath Our Feet* (Norwich: Canterbury Press, 2017), 150.
7. Taylor, *Altar in the World*, 151.

You also remember where you came from, and why. You touch the stuff your bones are made of. You handle the decomposed bodies of trees, leaves, birds, and fallen stars. Your body recognizes its kin. If you have nerve enough, you also force your own decomposition. This is not bad knowledge to have. It is the kind that puts other kinds in perspective. Feel that cool dampness? Welcome back to earth, you earthling. Smell that dirt? Welcome home, you beloved dust creature of God.[8]

Here we discover the eschatological dimension of an evolutionary theology that sees in the death and resurrection of Jesus Christ the future healing and transformation of the creation. This is the evangelistic aspect of an evolutionary Christian perspective—the gospel is about healing and restoration; it is about transformation and the possibility of new life. It is not about perfection or purity or human beings becoming something other than creatures; it is about the ways in which suffering and death lead to a new way of life—a new form of life in Jesus Christ. This is a message that young people need to hear—not that God is angry with them or God wants to judge them; God's anger and God's wrath are always directed at the distortion of created life when God's good creation becomes something it was never intended to be. Young people need to hear the message about God's relentless love that heals, restores, and makes new.

Embodied Spirituality

As the conversation between youth ministry and evolution deepens, it pushes us toward an embodied form of spirituality. In her book of *Franciscan Prayer*, Ilia Delio refers

8. Taylor, *Altar in the World*, 151.

to the "Franciscan path" of spirituality—a path that takes us down, back to our existence as creatures, as a way to encounter God. She writes, "Rather than fleeing the world to find God, God is to be found in the world.... The God whom Francis discovered in the cross of Jesus Christ was ... a God 'who delights to be with the simple and those rejected by the world.' Impressed by the love of the Crucified, Francis could no longer remain alone in his search for God. Rather, he had to find God in relation to the fragile creatureliness of the other: his neighbor, his brother, and yes, even the tiniest of creatures."[9] A deeper engagement of Saint Francis's radical call to poverty reveals it is about freedom—freeing ourselves from the systems and patterns that keep us trapped within ourselves. These systems always abstract identity; they point away from the diversity of creation, from the particularity of each person, in an attempt to name and control. When Francis strips himself of his earthly father's clothes and hands them back to him, at that moment he steps outside of every system, every reciprocal relationship, every political and economic attempt to gain power over someone or something else. Delio writes, "The encounter with Christ as other, therefore, imparted to Francis a new openness and freedom. Embraced by the compassionate love of God, Francis was liberated within and went out to embrace the other in love."[10]

Instead of emphasizing an ascent to God by overcoming the material, the spirituality of Saint Francis is a downward movement, following the movement of God who empties God's self in the incarnation of Jesus Christ, embracing created life, and becoming present with creation. For Fran-

---

9. Ilia Delio, *Franciscan Prayer* (Cincinnati, OH: St. Anthony Messenger Press, 2004), 62–63.
10. Delio, *Fanciscan Prayer*, 63.

cis, God is not found in abstracted spirituality or doctrinal principles; God is found in the face of the neighbor—the humanity of the neighbor that reveals the presence of Christ. Delio writes, "Prayer, therefore, is awakening to the presence of God in our lives. It is not a matter of climbing a ladder and 'going to God' but of realizing that God has 'come to us,' taking on our humanity. Christ is the pledge of God's love for us in 'whose embrace we are already caught up.'"

This approach to spirituality frees youth ministry from the desperate attempts to somehow make young people more "spiritual." Holiness does not exclude our humanity, and it is not some form of moral perfection; it means embracing God's love and choosing to live according to the law of love given to us in Jesus Christ. Young people do not need to be guilted into some unattainable prayer life, and they don't need to be shamed into an unsustainable devotional life—they need to encounter the love of God in the crucified and risen Christ who meets them in their humanity, in their frailty, and in their own particularity. God loves them because of their unique and strange differences, and God calls us to love each other in the same way.

This form of embodied spirituality transforms how we understand worship, how we pray, and how we read and interpret the Bible, and it invites us to include our bodies in the practices of spiritual formation. It transforms how we understand evangelism and mission by allowing us to encounter our brothers and sisters in their differences. This form of embodied spirituality calls us into a way of love where we encounter each other in mystery and awe and where we open ourselves to receive each other as a gift. Imagine how youth ministry could be transformed and the lives of our young people changed if the Christian community called young people out of the abstractions and the constant pressure toward progress—the nonstop pressure to be better, to be smarter, to be more moral, to become something. In the spirit of Saint Francis, youth ministry can, instead, invite them to embrace their humanity in the new humanity of Jesus Christ by inviting them to rest, to step outside of these unrealistic expectations and lay their anxieties, their fears, and their shame before the cross.

The Church

As a part of the course Science for Youth Ministry, I asked students to read the book *Anarchy Evolution: Faith, Science, and Bad Religion in a World without God* by Greg Graffin.[11] Graffin is a member of the band Bad Religion who now teaches biology at UCLA. He isn't a Christian, and he doesn't believe in God. I wanted students to read something from a different perspective, one that doesn't assume belief in a God as the creator of the cosmos. What's insightful about *Anarchy Evolution* is the way Graffin challenges both religion and science. He acknowledges that science can become just as fundamentalist as religion. He pushes back against the idea that natural selection is the driving force of evolution and isn't afraid to say that Darwin, though right on other things, was wrong on this issue. He also explains why he doesn't use the term *atheist* to define himself. Too often, atheists can be just as dogmatic as people who are religious, and as a punk rocker he pushes back against anyone who claims to be certain about anything.

Graffin's emphasis on creativity over creation focuses on the difference between a dynamic and static view of the

---

11. Greg Graffin and Steve Olson, *Anarchy Evolution: Faith, Science, and Bad Religion in a World without God* (New York: Harper Collins, 2010).

natural world. This resonates with the theological insights of Augustine, Aquinas, Julian of Norwich, and Bonaventure, who all see God's creative activity flowing as an act of divine love. In the incarnation, we discover the presence of God that opens up the possibility for something new in the death and resurrection of Jesus Christ. Here we discover hope that is grounded in the promise of a future. At the heart of the Christian faith is the gospel—a proclamation of freedom that becomes the basis for a new way of life. Which leads me to this final point: what would a punk rock youth ministry look like? What if youth ministry became a space where young people could ask questions that push against the tradition as it has been handed down to them? What if youth ministry became a space where young people could wrestle with the tradition, with the Bible, and with social and cultural issues with no fear of being reprimanded or labeled as heretical? What if youth pastors became theological scouts, entering into the unchartered territory of cultural issues and questions that are a part of the lived experience of young people in the West? Youth pastors need to become the interpretive guides on issues like science and faith, equipping young people to engage deep questions. In all of my discussions with young people, I sense that they are craving this type of spirituality, one that gives them something to hold on to as they wrestle with important questions. They need youth workers who are one part Saint Francis and one part punk rocker. People who are willing to direct young people to the crucified Christ, unloading all their baggage, so they can dance and sing, creatively living into their embodied spirituality by learning what it means to love God and love neighbor.

This punk rock youth ministry can also become a place to reclaim the practice of evangelism. I'm not talking about handing out tracts or asking anonymous people on the streets if they know if they would go heaven if they died today. I'm talking about a gospel-centered approach to evangelism that is all about the good news. Elaine Heath describes this approach to evangelism in her book *The Mystic Way of Evangelism: A Contemplative Vision for Christian Outreach.*[12] She approaches evangelism as a work of healing and restoration—an action that is always grounded in what she calls the hermeneutic of love. In the same way that God has emptied God's self in Jesus Christ, giving God's self for the healing of all creation, so too the Christian community must go outside of itself in love, becoming signs of God's healing transformation in the world. She tells the story of Sister Salvinette, a member of the group Missionary of Charity. The sisters live together in community, praying, worshiping, and doing life together, but their primary ministry is to meet the needs of the community. Sister Salvinette is clear that "prayer is the basis for their lives . . . the main thing they do," but it is this life of prayer that pushes them out into the community to meet Jesus in their neighbor.[13]

Heath describes the hesitancy of some young people in the church who are afraid that evangelism smacks of forcing our beliefs on others. She writes, "Sometimes my students think it is good to offer neighborly help as a form of evangelism. . . . But they are reluctant to tell those they are helping that they are doing it because of Jesus or the gospel. They think that offering such kindness in the name of Jesus is coercive toward those they help. This is, after all a pluralistic world. Sister Salvinette grew animated. 'We would never coerce anyone,' she said, 'but we always do these things for Jesus and we tell people about him.

---

12. Elaine A. Heath, *The Mystic Way of Evangelism: A Contemplative Vision for Christian Outreach* (Grand Rapids: Baker Academic, 2017).
13. Heath, *Mystic Way*, 113.

Remember, Jesus said that if we are ashamed of him before men, he will be ashamed of us before the Father!"[14]

Heath goes on to describe how so much outreach or evangelism is merely a way to protect our institutions. We want to get people to come to our church or to our youth group, so we come up with programming to keep our young people in or to get more to come. She writes, "Evangelism is mostly about strategies to keep newcomers from leaving for another church." She goes on to say, "The hermeneutic of love is grounded in the belief that Jesus really does live in the people around us, that Jesus thirsts in our actual neighbors. Jesus is bound with eternal love to every person I encounter."[15] This, according to Heath, changes things. It changes the way we think about church, about evangelism, and even about youth ministry. We are freed by the gospel to give ourselves for our neighbor with no regard for our institutions. Evangelism is not about making sure our youth ministry is the biggest, it's about shaping young people to live into the love of God revealed in Jesus Christ.

What would it look like for our youth ministers to cultivate true empathy? To develop practices and a way of life to help young people encounter the love of God in Jesus Christ? I've tried to show how an incarnational engagement of evolution can help young people get outside of themselves in a love of God that pushes them back to love the creation and their neighbor. It also helps young people recognize their own connection with the created world, that they are made to live as creatures, and that God loves them as human beings in Jesus Christ. This approach opens them up to seeing the creation as a dynamic community grounded in the love of the Trinity, a love that seeks our

---

14. Heath, *Mystic Way*, 113.
15. Heath, *Mystic Way*, 115.

healing and transformation. Such an approach refuses to be defined by fear—our identity is shaped not by what we are against but by who we are for. This approach to youth ministry frees young people from a life of anxiety and fear, opening them to the possibility of freedom and love for the world revealed in Jesus Christ. As the apostle Paul puts it in Romans 8:14–16: "For all who are led by the Spirit of God are children of God. For you did not receive a spirit of slavery to fall back into fear, but you have received a spirit of adoption. When we cry, 'Abba! Father!' it is that very Spirit bearing witness with our spirit that we are children of God."

I know what some of you are thinking. "This is all fine and well, and we might even agree with you, but how do we do this? Give us some practical examples." To which I reply—that's your job! Our responsibility as practitioners is to live this out, to embody it, within our own contexts and our own communities. This takes youth leaders who are curious, creative, and willing to explore the deeper questions of theology and science. It takes youth leaders who are willing to imagine what a conversation between science and faith looks like. It takes youth leaders who are courageous enough to ask the hard questions and give space for young people to wrestle with them. The foundation for this is already there in the things youth pastors already do, from mission trips to church camp, to teaching time, to worship. What's added to the mix is direction, meaning, and purpose, as well as a little bit of intentionality. At first it might seem challenging, but in the end, your young people and their parents will thank you for it.

Epilogue
Jason Lief

> Where were you when I laid the foundation of the earth?
> —Job 38:4

I close my Science for Youth Ministry course with Terrence Malick's film *The Tree of Life*. It's about a family living in Texas that tries to make sense of the unexpected death of a son. In the middle of the film, as the mother asks where God was when her son died, the film flashes back to the beginning moments of creation. The sequence includes the formation of stars, the earth, and the evolution of life. The nearly twenty-minute scene is God's wordless, Job-like, response to her question. I show the film to wrap up our discussion of science and faith because I want students to think about creation as an act of love. I also want students to understand that love and suffering are deeply connected. God demonstrates God's love for the world in the incarnation, taking on human flesh, and hanging from a cross. The crucifixion and resurrection of Jesus Christ is the climactic expression of divine love that brought forth creation in the beginning. I want students to consider that maybe evolution fits a cosmos created to express life, where death and suffering are part of a creation in which love is the ordering principle.

There needs to be a theological paradigm shift in the church to support the discussion between science and faith. The Christian community needs to help its members see the incarnation as God's love for the created world, and we need to help young people see the incarnation as an expression of God's love for their embodied lives. To do this, however, churches and their leaders need to be willing to have the conversation. We must be careful not to coerce people to believe the same things—Christians have differing views on origins, and it's important that the conversation be done with a spirit of generosity. The purpose of the conversation is to wrestle with the biblical story and with the theological beliefs the church has mined from it. At the same time, the church needs to allow members of the Christian community who engage in scientific research to show us how science and faith are not at odds. Regardless of where people eventually land on the origins issue, the church needs to help people see what the Bible actually says and what it doesn't say, while helping the community have a better understanding of what evolution says about the world.

There's no getting around the fact that this is a controversial topic, which makes the framing of the discussion all the more important. However, it's important to remember that at one time saying the earth revolved around the sun was just as controversial—something most Christians (I'm sure there are a few stubborn holdouts) now take as a matter of fact. Paradigm shifts take time. Scientific theories can disrupt the way people see and make sense of the world. With Augustine, however, we need to remember that the gospel is not tied to a particular metaphysic or scientific theory. Our task as the Christian community is to hear the good news within our social, cultural, and scientific context. God's word is strong enough to sustain any and all questions we bring to it; we do not need to fear, and the Bible does not need our protection. God wants us to read the Bible, again and again, with new and fresh eyes. Jesus tells his disciples again and again, "Do not let your hearts be troubled, and do not let them be afraid" (John

14:27). We don't need to fear evolution, and we certainly don't need to be afraid to talk about science and faith. Our hope is that this book has contributed in some small way to a healthy dialogue.

CPSIA information can be obtained
at www.ICGtesting.com
Printed in the USA
LVHW081253060919
630186LV00016B/380/P